A BETTER
HEART

A BETTER
HEART

— THE IMPACT OF —

CHRIST'S PURE LOVE

TOM CHRISTOFFERSON

**DESERET
BOOK**

Salt Lake City, Utah

DESERET BOOK is a registered trademark of Deseret Book Company.

Visit us at DeseretBook.com

Library of Congress Cataloging-in-Publication Data

CIP data on file
ISBN 978-1-62972-837-7

Printed in the United States of America
Lake Book Manufacturing, Inc., Melrose Park, IL

10   9   8   7   6   5   4   3   2   1

For Darius Gray,
a pathbreaker, guide, and mentor,

and for my Band of Brothers (and Sisters):
Todd & Kathy, Greg & MarJane, Tim & Julie, and Wade & Becky,

with gratitude, admiration, and love

CONTENTS

INTRODUCTION

Some time ago, a dear friend was dealing with a serious heart condition of arrhythmia. Initial procedures were tried without success. Finally her physician, a cardiac electrophysiologist, performed an intricate procedure, followed by a new course of medication. At the one-year mark post-procedure, the doctor believed he could declare a success in managing the condition. My friend asked her doctor, "So how is it that my heart has a completely new rhythm?" He answered: "The heart is a miraculous organ. The procedure I performed changed some of the tissue of your heart. In the process of healing, your heart has literally reformed itself." An echocardiogram confirmed the results. Her heart had dramatically changed. The cardiac intervention and medication *each day* improved her heart until a new heart established and maintained a healthy rhythm on its own.

The physical experience of my friend and the medical care she received has a parallel in our spiritual lives. The Master Physician cares for us and will change our spiritual hearts to work in rhythm with His. As we understand the love Jesus Christ has for us and our love for Him, and as we study and seek His precious gift of charity, we begin the daily process toward fashioning a better heart.

One summer evening, in a beautiful canyon setting during a family reunion, the adults were gathered for conversation. One of my brothers observed that, while gifts of the Spirit are separately provided that all may communally profit, charity is one spiritual gift that everyone may obtain, and indeed that each one of us should seek.

That insight and counsel captured my mind, and it has been the impetus for more than a decade of study and exploration. It has provided a wonderful reason to dig deeper and to be more observant of those around me who exhibit this virtue. Although today the word *charity* is often taken to mean giving money or other help to those in need, the more profound meaning the Lord attaches to this gift is much richer and, in fact, eternal in scope.

Mormon describes charity as "the pure love of Christ" (Moroni 7:47). Reading in the synoptic Gospels and Third Nephi, we can see what His love looks like for the people among whom He ministered while on this earth. I am particularly drawn to the Apostle John, who memorably describes himself on several occasions as the disciple "whom Jesus loved." Uniquely found in his Gospel, or testimony, is the experience of Jesus, "having loved his own which were in the world, he loved them unto the end" (John 13:1), washing the feet of His disciples. In this act of subservience, Jesus taught, "If I then, your Lord and Master, have washed your feet; ye also ought to wash one another's feet" (John 13:14). That gesture encompasses the outward expression of charity: His love is for our spirits, our hearts, as well as for our physical needs, our feet. For those who do not as yet know Him, He sends us to emit and reflect His love for *their* hearts and *their* feet. And as we seek His gift of charity, and our hearts align with His, each of us may humbly consider ourselves disciples whom Jesus loves. We may with gratitude recognize that in His service we are in the process of becoming as He is, each day gaining a better heart, one in rhythm with His.

In Alma's superlative sermon on faith, he spoke of a willingness to believe, even simply a desire to believe, as the necessary first step. "But behold, if ye will awake and arouse your faculties, even to an experiment upon my words, and exercise a particle of faith, yea, even if ye can no more than desire to believe, let this desire work in you, even until ye believe in a manner that ye can give place for a portion of my words" (Alma 32:27). I believe the same process applies to our desire to gain all the gifts of the Spirit that the Lord sees fit to provide to us. In this case, a *desire* to be filled with Christ's spiritual gift of charity is the necessary first step. Through the pages of this book, I invite you to join me in seeking to learn more deeply, as adapted to the individual circumstances of your life, as you desire, pray, work, and obtain a better heart.

PART ONE

CHRIST'S LOVE FOR US

CHAPTER ONE

HE TAUGHT OF HIS LOVE

No creature is so lowly,
No sinner so depraved,
But feels thy presence holy,
And thru thy love is saved.
Tho craven friends betray thee,
They feel thy love's embrace;
The very foes who slay thee
Have access to thy grace.

—Karen Lynn Davidson, "O Savior, Thou Who Wearest a Crown" (*Hymns*, no. 197)

Come, sit at my table! I love to cook for friends and family. Cleaning up afterward? Not so much. I enjoy paging through an exquisitely photographed book of recipes. Much like a travel guide that whets my appetite for adventure and learning in a new location, a cookbook inspires me with new ideas for elements to make a meal memorable. Over time I have collected and given away many cookbooks to share the pleasure and the experience of good food. When I read through a recipe, I imagine obtaining and combining the ingredients; at times, while reading the preparation instructions for a new dish, it is almost as if I can taste the finished product. And yet, as wonderful as that journey of imagination is, reading the recipe doesn't give the experience that comes from trial and error in the kitchen. And it certainly doesn't provide any nutrition!

Experiencing Christ's presence through the scriptures, though necessary and helpful, can be like imagining the taste of food while reading a recipe: it is wonderfully satisfying, but even better is to make the visualization real. Through the gift of the Holy Spirit, more than simply reading, we can experience the proffer our Savior has made: "And ye see that I have commanded that none of you should go away, but rather have commanded that ye should come unto me, that ye might feel and see; even so shall ye do unto the world; and whosoever breaketh this commandment suffereth himself to be led into temptation" (3 Nephi 18:25).

With the assistance of the Spirit, as we contemplate the love of Christ for us, as we read of His engagement with others in the Gospels and Third Nephi, you and I can visualize in our minds what it must have felt like to be near Him. We might imagine seeing through the eyes of Mary and Joseph as Jesus grows in stature, grace for grace, experiencing His increasing knowledge of His divine mission, the path He alone will be able to walk. We sit with Him in a moment and place as He tutors His Apostles—as they struggle to learn and understand, we witness His patience and compassion. We place ourselves in the shoes of Mary and Martha as He comforts them after Lazarus's death, before performing the miracle of restored life, and as they feel both His touch and His tears. We picture being among the Nephites, hearing Him commune with heaven, overflowing with "the joy which filled our souls at the time we heard him pray for us unto the Father" (3 Nephi 17:17).

A friend once quoted a nutrition instructor as saying, "We often hear that we are what we eat, but that isn't true—what matters is what we absorb!" We can read and marvel at the words of holy scripture, but until the teachings and doctrines penetrate us, until we absorb

4

what the Lord is teaching, we limit the words of apostles and prophets, ancient and modern, to being simply wonderful moral teaching. As Elder D. Todd Christofferson said, "I suppose that never in history has a people been blessed with such a quantity of holy writ. And not only that, but every man, woman, and child may possess and study his or her own personal copy of these sacred texts, most in his or her own language" ("The Blessing of Scripture," *Ensign*, May 2010).

That blessing of a significant quantity of readily available scripture won't change our hearts simply by its existence. Rather, when we desire and invite the Spirit to tutor our souls, and we make real efforts ourselves, then we can absorb what the Lord desires to teach us through all the sources of His holy word, including personal revelation.

The spiritual learning process often entails challenges, even frustration, as we work to fully understand and absorb doctrines that at first blush appear simple. As a Master Teacher, Jesus used parables in His ministry to aid His listeners in discerning His meaning. In addition, they were a method of providing layers of meaning that could be envisioned and comprehended through exposure over and over again through time. Each parable also provides ways that we can learn more of Him, to discover His true character—which is in every measure a perfect reflection of His Father's—so that we can better know and love both God the Son and God the Father.

Parables are one tool the Lord uses as He invites us to learn of Him: "Take my yoke upon you, and learn of me; for I am meek and lowly in heart: and ye shall find rest unto your souls" (Matthew 11:29).

The parable we normally think of as the story of the Prodigal Son (see Luke 15:11–32) could more helpfully be titled the story of The

Righteous Father of Two Sons. We can learn of Christ in His role of Father as the Creator of this earth, as the Head of those who have accepted His gospel, and as the One who has made possible our resurrection—our spiritual rebirth and physical salvation.

The Merriam-Webster online dictionary provides several definitions of the word *prodigal*. The first two connote the way we normally think of the younger son in the story: "characterized by profuse or wasteful expenditure" and "recklessly spendthrift." But the third definition describes the father: "yielding abundantly" (https://www.merriam-webster.com/dictionary/prodigal). So we could also, with that abundance in mind, call this the parable of the Prodigal Father.

The portrait Jesus provides us of this family is necessarily broad. We know nothing of the life either son had led prior to the younger son's desire to depart. We have no insight into the thoughts and expectations of this younger son, so the image we have of him at the outset is unidimensional. All we initially learn is that he wasted his substance with riotous living.

As Karen Lynn Davidson so poignantly expressed in the lines that began this chapter, no one is so lowly or depraved as to have lost the ability to recognize the Holy Divine. Intuitively we understand that when *every* knee shall bow and *every* tongue confess that Jesus is indeed the Living Son of the Living God, many of those tongues will have before that moment been much more accustomed to profane His name. When many of those knees will have bowed in the past, it will have been to him who falsely proclaims himself the ruler of this world. And, at some moment or another, haven't we been counted among them? Can we feel at least some kinship with that younger son?

6

A friend and scholar, David Butler, has said that when the younger son asks, while his father yet lives, for the share of property that would be his upon the death of his father, he is saying in effect, "I wish you were dead" (David Butler and Emily Belle Freeman, *Don't Miss This,* podcast video, April 29, 2019; https://youtu.be/WwnCotAkIaA). And yet the father apparently liquidates assets to accomplish what this seemingly unkind and ungrateful son has requested. Have you and I never wanted a reward before it was fully due? The first lesson the parable teaches us about Christ as Father is that He acts in love toward us even when our love for Him has grown cold. (And a second lesson could be that we should exercise caution in what we ask of Him, because He might comply!)

As Jesus unfolds the story of the downward spiral of this son's life, He includes an element that would have had eloquent meaning to His contemporary audience. The Mosaic law had declared pigs unclean, and now that this son was living among the pigs, he had effectively become one of them. When this penniless and now also unclean son "comes to himself" and determines to ask to be a servant in his father's employ, we gain another lesson in the character of Christ as Father. It is, finally, his father's *goodness* that calls this son home.

Another image of Christ as Father occurs as we envision this abundant, generous, loving patriarch standing at his window watching the road with hope and faith that his son will return; perhaps he spends days on the high point of his land searching, ever searching, for that longed-for moment when he who is lost will come home. In the words of Elder Jeffrey R. Holland: "The tender image of this boy's anxious, faithful father running to meet him and showering him with kisses is one of the most moving and compassionate scenes in all of holy writ. It tells every child of God, wayward or otherwise, how much God wants us back in the protection of His arms" ("The Other Prodigal," *Ensign*, May 2002).

That the father does not wait for the son to reach him, nor walk at the stately pace of a man of prominence, but runs to bathe with his tears he who was lost is another lesson of Christ as Father: He is always eager to welcome any approach we make to Him; He is ever watchful, ever joyful when we seek Him.

To let this truth sink deep, let's think for a moment of the converse, the antithesis of this father's unqualified love. Perhaps in those unholy years of junior high school you had the experience of seeing fellow students shun others because they feared that their own social standing could be diminished if they were seen to be too friendly, too kind to those stamped "uncool." Were you the shunner, were you the shunned, were you the silent observer, uncomfortable but inert? Like me, in various circumstances and times, you probably fit each role. So we know how easy, how human it is to parse a meager dosage of love that is absolutely conditional upon our view of the merits of the recipient.

This father, though—this type and symbol of Christ the Father— provides an eager and tender welcome, and he does it before the son has ever opened his mouth. This father has not waited to hear confessions, repentant words, proclamations of regret, and pleas for forgiveness. This father never lets his son beg for the opportunity to become his servant. This son, with faults and errors aplenty (a symbol and type of each of us), is received by his father as a son and once again as an heir. Christ as Father likewise cloaks us with His perfect love, bestows forgiveness and mercy hard-won in the Garden of Gethsemane and on the cross of Calvary, upon any indication of penance and any desire to become better. Can there be a more profound way to demonstrate that His love is unqualified, and that <u>when a heart is</u> <u>changed, the past is forgotten and a glorious inheritance unfolds?</u>

When the older son appears in the story, we learn even more of the greatness and character of the father. He turns away the misplaced anger of this son with soft, tender words, words we all pray to hear someday: "Thou art ever with me, and all that I have is thine" (Luke 15:31). Of course, a most wonderful thing we know about our Heavenly Father and Christ as Father is that each would as accurately give the same glorious benediction and promise to the younger son as well.

As I read of the reaction of the older son upon hearing the sounds of rejoicing and merriment, and perhaps smelling the fatted calf on the spit, I am reminded of an experience I had as a college student babysitting some of my nieces and nephews when their parents had gone out for the evening. One niece, about four or five years old at the time, had developed the habit of prolonging the inevitable bedtime for as long as possible. I had sent all the children upstairs to bed and was washing dishes and cleaning the kitchen. This niece appeared several times, needing a drink of water, having a question, requesting another story. Finally, I told her quite firmly to *go to bed.* She sat on the bottom tread of the stairs wailing for a while and finally went to her room. After it had been quiet for about half an hour, I tiptoed to her room to see what she was doing. When I reached her bed, I could see that she had her arms tightly folded across her chest, with her lower lip pushed out in a pout—and she was fast asleep!

It's easy to hold on to frustration, as my niece did that night, and as the elder brother in the parable seemed to do. If each of us can recall moments in our lives when we were in the position of the younger son, I expect we can also think of times when we were in the shoes of the older one. Don't we all want to be acknowledged for our good work? For our loyalty and dependability? Do we occasionally twist a little inside when the spotlight shines on those who have done less, or for a shorter time, or with fewer obstacles in front of them? Or perhaps we have become accustomed to being shown respect and appreciation for our faithfulness, and we feel justified in expecting others to recognize our contributions. It is as if the cameras on the smartphones of our lives are in permanent "selfie" mode, always reversed to face us rather than to capture the world about us.

We may even feel that we demonstrate our loyalty, in this case to the father, by our poor treatment of those we feel have demeaned him. When I was ten or eleven years old, our family lived in Glenview, Illinois. Across the street from us had lived a mother and daughter who had joined the Church soon after we moved there, but who had now moved to Hawaii. A father and his rather unruly sons had moved in.

One day my mother mentioned that one of the boys had made a rude gesture with one finger and said something unkind as she backed out of our driveway. A few days later, one of these boys knocked on our door and, when I answered, asked if he could borrow some sugar (as I recall). I dismissively told him that because they had disrespected my mother, I wouldn't give them anything. When Mother returned home that day, I was eager to tell her how I had stood up for her honor. She looked at me with sad eyes and said, "Oh, I think they have a challenging life, and if they need food, we always want to help." I instantly went from feeling that I had been her stalwart defender to realizing that I had instead disappointed her. When I went across the street bringing sugar, I was curtly told they no longer needed it, and a relationship that might have been helpful to all involved was stillborn. That memory haunts me still.

The lesson I learned from my mother was not simply that we should always share our food with those in need, but, of greater importance, that poor conduct by another does not give us dispensation to respond in kind. Jesus taught that a disciple will turn the other cheek, will go a second mile, will "give to him that asketh thee, and from him that would borrow of thee turn not thou away" (Matthew 5:42). My mother heard in the Master's call the opportunity to grow in love, even for those who initially saw her in a less gracious light.

And so, what becomes apparent in this parable is that although the older son may love his father, love has not been the motivation for his work and effort. In his world, dividing the wealth is a zero-sum game—anything for his brother means less for himself. To again quote Elder Holland:

> One who has heretofore presumably been very happy with his life and content with his good fortune suddenly feels very unhappy simply because another has had some good fortune as well.
>
> Who is it that whispers so subtly in our ear that a gift given to another somehow diminishes the blessings we have received? Who makes us feel that if God is smiling on another, then He surely must somehow be frowning on us? You and I both know who does this—it is the father of all lies. ("The Other Prodigal")

What did the older son think should be the reward for his labors, for being the faithful, stayed-at-home son? Whatever it was, in some measure it would be insufficient in his eyes were it also to be given to his brother. He seems to have placed his belief in a gospel of scarcity.

We learn of Christ as Father that His love is never lessened because it is equally bestowed. Every recipient is invited to gain all that His Father has to give. We learn that His willingness to forgive, His grace to meet us where we are and lift us toward Him, and His mercy and compassion are fully available to every one of us. We learn that His goodness is without limit, a well that will never run dry. There is no grading curve: for one to gain eternal life does not mean that another one, or one thousand, must receive a lesser glory. Eternal life, which is a description of the quality rather than the duration of God's life, is not a zero-sum game. There is only abundance in His home. Christ the Father's goal and purpose is that every single individual born to mortal life will return and be exalted, to enjoy the kind of life that He enjoys, forever.

Let us learn of Him.

Another parable with direct application to our understanding of the character of Christ is the story of the Good Samaritan. John Dummelow has observed:

> The "lawyer" intended to justify himself by showing that, even upon a liberal interpretation of the word "neighbour," he had done his duty. He expected Christ to say that a neighbour was a friend or at least an Israelite. The idea that a "neighbour" might be a foreigner had never occurred to him. . . . "We are not to contrive the death of the Gentiles, but if they are in any danger of death we are not bound to deliver them, e.g. if any of them fall into the sea you need not take him out, for such a one is not thy neighbour."

In answer Christ appealed to the man's conscience, not to his reason. If Christ had said "a heathen is thy neighbour," the man would have argued the point with learned subtlety. Instead of this Jesus told him a story in which a man treated a foreigner as a neighbour, and the lawyer was bound to confess that this was in accordance with the mind of God. ("A Commentary on the Holy Bible: Complete in One Volume with General Articles" [January 1970], Luke 10, retrieved from studylight.org)

As we read Jesus's teaching through this parable, we can place ourselves in the position of each character in the story, as well as that of the lawyer who asks the question that precipitates the parable, in order to better understand what is being taught.

Are we ever that lawyer, hoping to find justification to avoid doing things we feel we probably should but definitely don't want to do? Do I minister only to those to whom I am assigned, or even only to those of the assigned with whom I feel some affinity? Do my children feel my love only when they are obedient?

Are we ever the priest, so intent on fulfilling our church obligations that we pass by those whom the Savior has put in our way? In order to be a priest in Israel, one had to be the son of a priest, and pure in mind and body. Each time he entered the temple, he would be examined to ensure his purity. In Numbers 19, we learn that the priest must avoid corpse impurity—touching or even raising his hand over a dead or dying body. Those listening to Jesus teach might not have been surprised that the priest passed the sufferer by.

Are we ever the Levite, letting the concerns of our work, our daily schedule, allow us to pass by one in need, hoping perhaps that someone else with less time pressure will stop? Levites were the lower order of priests in the temple; the rules of purity for them were less strict. The audience for Jesus's story might have begun to feel a little uncomfortable at the Levite's inaction.

Do we invite into our homes those who are unlike us, from different cultures, countries, or religions, in order that our children can learn what borderless respect, acceptance, and empathy look and feel like? Doing what Jesus would do is an eloquent way of teaching without words.

My friend and confidante Carol Lynn Pearson penned a timeless verse for the *Children's Songbook*:

> *If you don't walk as most people do,*
> *Some people walk away from you,*
> *But I won't! I won't! . . .*
> *I'll walk with you. I'll talk with you.*
> *That's how I'll show my love for you.*
> *Jesus walked away from none.*
> *He gave His love to ev'ryone.*
> *So I will! I will!*
> *Jesus blessed all he could see,*
> *Then turned and said, "Come, follow me."*
> *And I will! I will! I will! I will!*
> *I'll walk with you. I'll talk with you.*
> *That's how I'll show my love for you.*
> ("I'll Walk with You," *Children's Songbook*, 140.
> Used with permission)

Recently, in a children's picture book, *I'll Walk with You*, Carol Lynn has added more examples: "If you don't look as some people do," "If you don't pray as some people pray," and "If you don't love as some people do." Each way of expanding the manifestation of difference allows us to focus again on what never changes: "Jesus blessed all he could see, Then turned and said, 'Come, follow me.'"

As the COVID-19 virus made its appearance around the world and seemingly stopped many of us in our tracks, those in the health professions doubled their efforts to heal and to comfort—with compassion recognizing that, at some times, theirs was the only loving face an individual might see. I was touched by family and friends who checked in frequently to ensure I was physically well and mentally healthy. Their solicitude became a reminder that there were many to whom I ought to be extending the same tender kindliness. I learned that I don't even have to be busy in order to pass by without pausing to aid another in need: I render myself sightless as I create a cocoon of my own cares.

Returning to the parable of the Good Samaritan, are we ever the Samaritan? Rather than self-centering on how others view us, do we seek rather to identify need around us and use whatever talents and abilities we have to alleviate suffering? Sister Sharon Eubank, speaking in general conference, offered support and empathy for each of us as we deal with grief, fatigue, feelings that we don't "fit," or unanswered questions. Citing our need for friends and for the loving assistance we gain from one another, Sister Eubank also encouraged us to add the gifts and abilities we have in unity with others:

> Our individual light may be like only one light bulb on
> a tree. But we still shine our small light, and all together, like
> Temple Square at Christmastime, we attract millions of people
> to the house of the Lord. Best of all, as President Nelson has

encouraged, we can bring the Savior's light to ourselves and the people important to us by the simple act of keeping our covenants. In a variety of ways, the Lord rewards that faithful act with power and with joy.

I testify you are beloved. The Lord knows how hard you are trying. You are making progress. Keep going. He sees all your hidden sacrifices and counts them to your good and the good of those you love. Your work is not in vain. You are not alone. His very name, Emmanuel, means "God with us." He is surely with you. ("Christ: The Light That Shines in Darkness," *Ensign*, May 2019)

He invites: Come, learn of Me.

As we consider the parable of the Good Samaritan, beyond what it may teach us about ourselves or invite us to do, we also see types and symbols of Jesus Christ. Just as the journey from Jerusalem to Jericho meant going from a high place to a low one, Jesus descended from His heavenly home in order to become the Son of Man of Holiness on earth. Like the Samaritan, He was "despised and rejected of men; a man of sorrows, and acquainted with grief" (Isaiah 53:3). And like the Samaritan, Jesus has saved us: "And Jesus said unto him, This day is salvation come to this house. . . . For the Son of man is come to seek and to save that which was lost" (Luke 19:9–10). As the Samaritan used oil and wine for healing, Jesus gives us power to consecrate oil for healing and is Himself the Living Water symbolized by water in our sacrament of the Lord's Supper. Rather than bringing us to an inn, Christ brings us to His Father's house, where, if we are willing, each of us can become like a child at home in the one home that is our birthright. Above all, He has paid the price, not simply for bed and watch care, but for our sins. He has experienced our sorrows and suffering and has loosed the bands of death in order that He may succor us (see Alma 7:12).

As through His grace He acts forever as the Good Samaritan, so are we continually the wounded traveler on the side of the road, in need of care we cannot provide for ourselves. We will be injured in our journey through this life—it is an essential part of our learning process here. This is not because the Lord is unwilling to spare us pain. Rather, He is unwilling to shield us from those moments that will cause us to reach to Him, when He alone can be our strength and solace. Those times when we most want to shake our fists at heaven because of sorrow, agony, and discouragement are the very instants when we ought to drop to our knees. We kneel in gratitude for Him who knows each difficulty in every detail as vividly as we do, and in supplication for His continued compassionate care.

> Because God wants us to come home after having become more like Him and His Son, part of this developmental process, of necessity, consists of showing unto us our weaknesses. Hence, if we have ultimate hope we will be submissive, because with His help, those weaknesses can even become strengths.
>
> It is not an easy thing, however, to be shown one's weaknesses, as these are regularly demonstrated by life's circumstances. Nevertheless, this is part of coming unto Christ, and it is a vital, if painful, part of God's plan of happiness. Besides, as Elder Henry B. Eyring has wisely observed, "If you want praise more than instruction, you may get neither." (Neal A. Maxwell, "Hope through the Atonement of Jesus Christ," *Ensign*, November 1998)

Challenges and corrections from Him reflect Christ's love for us and His desire that we might fully realize all the gifts and strengths that He sees in us. When we truly understand this, our hearts really do change, and in increasing measure we come to want for ourselves exactly what He desires.

A noted theologian, Dr. N. T. Wright, has taught:

> God's love is like a circle; and a circle is endless. Whom God loves, he loves to the end; and his end is, not that he should cease to love them; no: his end is, to love them still . . . Jesus, having loved his own who were in the world, loved them to the uttermost. . . . There is no point in a doctor coming to live with her patients and catch their diseases without having the medicine to deal with them. There is no point in a music teacher coming to a class of tuneless children and merely joining in their cacophony. There is no point in a shepherd lying down alongside the sheep when he should be leading them to fresh water and then urging them into the sheepfold because there's a wolf on the prowl. ("The Circle of Love," Sermon at the Ordination of Deacons in Durham Cathedral, June 27, 2010)

The theme and message of all scripture is that Jesus is the medicine, the Master Physician. He is the notes and chords, He is Living Water and Bread of Life, He is the Good Shepherd.

In the parables we have examined, the Righteous Father with Two Sons and the Good Samaritan, we have endeavored to come and learn of Him. We have seen that His desire to share with us everything His Father has is not conditional; rather it is unchanging and forever. That divine desire is not diminished by our folly, although we are allowed to shut our doors to it. He will continue to knock for as long as we wish to hide in the shadows. His holy call is to higher action. He aims to persuade us to return kindness for meanness, to replace apathy with rapt attention to others, to discard the need for praise from peers in order to hear the silent "well done" He communicates through the Spirit. His character is one of abundance; our small steps are met with outsize blessings. "Give, and it shall be given unto you; good measure, pressed down, and shaken together, and running over, shall men give into your bosom" (Luke 6:38).

His prophets before His birth and after His Resurrection, as well as He Himself, have taught us the most essential distillation of His character: that love, for His Father and for each of us, undermines and infuses His every thought and action, the two great commandments performed perfectly and infinitely.

CHAPTER TWO

HE SHOWED US LOVE

Oh, love effulgent, love divine!
What debt of gratitude is mine,
That in his off'ring I have part
And hold a place within his heart.

—Edward P. Kimball, "God Loved Us, So He Sent His Son" (*Hymns*, no. 187)

I live near Phoenix, Arizona. In an average year, the area will receive about eight to nine inches of rain, which is about one-fifth the national average in the United States. In the summertime, we periodically get what are locally called monsoon rains. Now, I've been in India during the monsoon season there, and I've never seen so much water come out of the sky. It goes on and on! Our local monsoons aren't even close to that. The summer rain in the Phoenix area is often preceded by dust storms and high winds; then the rains come down heavily, but relatively briefly. The smell after a summer storm is heavenly; the hot, dry desert air instantly becomes sweet. And after a very wet season during our winter, the Sonoran desert near Phoenix quickly becomes a riot of color. I mention this because living in Arizona—which is quite different from my former home in lush, green New England—gives a sense of how immediately rain changes a landscape, how new growth can appear almost as you watch. Our souls blossom that quickly too as we feel the love of Christ for each one of us as individuals.

The very first time Joseph Smith recorded the experience we call the First Vision, in 1832, much of it in his own handwriting, he wrote something I find powerfully compelling. These words follow his description of the content of the vision: "My soul was filled with love and for many days I could rejoice with great Joy and the Lord was with me" ("History, circa Summer 1832," p. 3, The Joseph Smith Papers; https://www.josephsmithpapers.org/paper-summary/history-circa-summer-1832/3).

Parents can often describe one particularly vivid memory of a joyful moment with a child in a twinkling flash of thought: "I never want her to grow; I want this instant to be frozen in time." That has been my feeling as well after precious points when I have become fully aware of Christ's knowledge of me and luxuriated in the feeling of His love. Absorbing it, I want to savor and relish it. I want to hold the impression tightly and never return to the ordinariness of daily life.

It is significant to me that the Apostle John names himself as "one of his [Jesus's] disciples, whom Jesus loved" (John 13:23; see also 19:26; 21:20), and he is the same, we presume, who said, "We love him, because he first loved us" (1 John 4:19). I hope that you have had or will have an epiphany, a manifestation to you of His adoration of you. After all, He did what none other could, not for humanity in general, but through an atoning experience that allowed Him to redeem *you*—such that you would want to refer to yourself as "the one whom He loves."

The great Book of Mormon prophets before Jesus's time on earth understood that His offering represents love. When Nephi desires to understand the vision that his father, Lehi, has been shown, he receives a vision of his own and is able to carry on a conversation with the angel who appears to him. As he is shown Mary and her newborn Son, the angel tells him:

> Behold the Lamb of God, yea, even the Son of the Eternal Father! Knowest thou the meaning of the tree which thy father saw?
>
> And I answered him, saying: Yea, it is the love of God, which sheddeth itself abroad in the hearts of the children of men; wherefore, it is the most desirable above all things.
>
> And he spake unto me, saying: Yea, and the most joyous to the soul. . . .
>
> And it came to pass that I beheld that the rod of iron, which my father had seen, was the word of God, which led to the fountain of living waters, or to the tree of life; which waters are a representation of the love of God; and I also beheld that the tree of life was a representation of the love of God. (1 Nephi 11:21–23, 25)

As Nephi now understood, every symbol and action of Jesus ultimately portrays His love.

We have the opportunity to see how Jesus demonstrated His love as we observe His interactions with those whom society demeaned, people who were trying to cope with some of the greatest challenges of their lives. It sounds a little strange to say it, but I really love the story of the woman caught in the act of adultery in the New Testament. Of course, the story raises many questions: Why was the man with whom she acted not also brought forward to be judged? (It is almost unbearable to imagine that he might stealthily have joined the crowd of her accusers.) Was the whole thing set up as yet another attempt to trap Jesus? How did these men even know where to go looking for this unfortunate woman?

We should recognize that we have not been given specific knowledge of the circumstances of the case, whether she participated by her own choice or if, in some fashion, she had been forced into a situation that violated her agency. That lack of information should give us pause before we immediately conclude that she has sinned. We should also recognize at the outset that the historical mix-up of Mary of Magdala, Mary of Bethany, and an unnamed woman who anoints Jesus's feet with oil, beginning hundreds of years after the Magdalene's death, has confused, perhaps even tainted, the portrait of the woman who appears often in the Gospels as a faithful and important disciple and is the first to see her risen Messiah.

You know the story: those who accused the woman were much less interested in either her guilt or her innocence, let alone the possibility of her redemption; rather, they saw a wonderfully convenient opportunity to trap Jesus. They expected if Jesus acceded to the Mosaic law (which punishment should, by the way, have been carried out against both the woman and the man involved), He would become complicit in her death. However, if He urged mercy, He would not be upholding the spiritual law. Biblical scholar Frederic Farrar explained:

> They thought that now they had caught Him in a dilemma. They knew the divine trembling pity which had loved where others hated, and praised where others scorned, and encouraged where others crushed; and they knew how that pity had won for Him the admiration of many, the passionate devotion of not a few. They knew that a publican was among His chosen,

that sinners had sat with Him at the banquet, and harlots unre-proved had bathed His feet, and listened to His words. Would He then acquit this woman, and so make Himself liable to an accusation of heresy, by placing Himself in open disaccord with the sacred and fiery Law? or, on the other hand, would He belie His own compassion, and be ruthless, and condemn? And, if He did, would He not at once shock the multitude, who were touched by His tenderness, and offend the civil magistrates by making Himself liable to a charge of sedition? How could He possibly get out of the difficulty? Either alternative—heresy or treason, accusation before the Sanhedrin or delation to the Procurator, opposition to the orthodox or alienation from the many—would serve equally well their unscrupulous intentions. And one of these, they thought, must follow. What a happy chance this . . . woman had given them!

But the spirit which actuated these Scribes and Pharisees was not by any means the spirit of a sincere and outraged purity. In the decadence of national life, in the daily familiarity with heathen degradations, in the gradual substitution of a Levitical scrupulosity for a heartfelt religion, the morals of the nation had grown utterly corrupt . . . and the death by stoning as a punish-ment for adultery had long been suffered to fall into desuetude. Not even the Scribes and Pharisees—for all their external religi-osity—had any genuine horror of an impurity with which their own lives were often stained. . . .

And, therefore, to subject her to the superfluous horror of this odious publicity—to drag her, fresh from the agony of de-tection, into the sacred precincts of the Temple—to subject this unveiled, dishevelled, terror-stricken woman to the cold and sensual curiosity of a malignant mob—to make her, with total disregard to her own sufferings, the mere passive instrument of their hatred against Jesus; and to do all this—not under the pressure of moral indignation, but in order to gratify a calculating malice—showed on their parts a cold, hard cynicism, a graceless, pitiless, barbarous brutality of heart and conscience, which could not but prove, in every particular, revolting and hateful to One who alone was infinitely tender, because He alone was infinitely pure. (*The Life of Christ* [Minneapolis, MN: Klock & Klock Christian Publisher, 1982], 328–29)

There are messages I draw from this story that clearly show me His love in action, and in a most difficult circumstance. And isn't that exactly the circumstance in which true character, let alone courage, is revealed? First, before anything else, He acted to save the woman's life. His challenge to her accusers to examine their own consciences silenced them immediately as they considered: were they in a position to righteously judge? Each was convicted, and each slipped quietly away.

Second, He neither berated nor castigated. He came to her in her moment of greatest despair and need, having drawn the hostile attention away from her toward Himself. Now alone with her, He honored her with simple candor, helping her see where she stood in that moment—"where are those thine accusers? hath no man condemned thee?" (John 8:10).

Third, and finally, He gave her hope. Implicit in His charge, "go, and sin no more," was confidence in her capacity to do so. It demonstrated His expectation of her ability to act rather than to be acted upon, His knowledge that she had within herself the resources and faith to do so. She would have the opportunity, as do we all, to recognize the goodness within her that He saw and to turn her life in a direction that would ultimately lead to His presence. The circumstances of her life in that society may have made it very difficult for her to follow His counsel, but because He honors desires as well as actions, her soul could be aligned with His grace.

This woman's awful reality may be different in substance from mine—the immediacy of life-ending punishment has not been within my experience—but can I see myself as any more worthy or any less desperate for His succor? It is clear that there are no circumstances in my life or yours that would place us beyond His ability—and willingness—to reach and to show to us the same compassion, hope, and patience that He conveyed to this woman. Can we, then, do any less in our own engagement with brothers and sisters, whatever may be the challenges in their lives, however little we may understand their circumstances? Will we act first to save a life? Will we reach those in need where they are, and offer hope? Will we convey His love and help them know that they are enough, that their desires to do better are already a wonderful step toward a changed and better heart?

I have always felt an affinity for the Samaritan woman at Jacob's Well. Her thorny life, her near-immediate recognition of the Messiah, and her urgent missionary efforts beckon my heart. I hope I can be as perceptive, as faithful, as courageous as she. Clearly, Jesus's visit with her did not occur by accident. His appearance at midday when she would come alone to fetch water allowed Him to share with her, and all of us, His message of Living Water. I feel such love for her, especially because when Jesus lets her know that He knows about the difficulties in her life (five earlier husbands and a current companion to whom she is not married), her immediate reaction is not to rationalize or justify. I'm guessing life could be hard for a single widow in Samaria, that the help of her companion might have been all that kept a roof over her head. It might have been tempting to try to explain, but rather, she simply states her recognition that He is a prophet. As their conversation culminates in Christ's first clear declaration in His earthly ministry of His divine role, nothing else matters to her, not even the water jug she has come to fill. She does not quietly hold to herself the knowledge that Messiah has come, but runs to her village to testify and share what she has learned with others. Jesus then spends two days teaching and converting these people whom the Jews considered Gentiles. His love has opened new possibilities in the woman's life and in the lives of a whole village.

In my mind's eye, I see an older woman whose face and figure show the effects of hard years, one who has had to make her own way in an indifferent world, and yet whose heart is not cankered by a life that hasn't unfolded as she could have wished. It was not deemed appropriate in that society and that time for a single man to be alone with a woman, and yet when she arrives in the heat of the day to fill yet another jug of water, Jesus is waiting to change her life. As I envision the scene, I feel so clearly His love for her, for her innate goodness, in spite of all that life has thrown at her. I long to meet her someday.

My mind also turns to all those whom Jesus healed, as well as the three He raised back to life. The woman with an issue of blood, lepers, the paralytic at the pool of Bethesda, the blind, the mother of Peter's wife, an infirm woman, a deaf mute, one with dropsy, a man with a withered hand, and those who had been troubled by evil spirits. Would not each of these individuals have felt Christ's love as well as His power in their miraculous healing?

The book of Third Nephi in the Book of Mormon with majestic clarity shows us a Redeemer whose heart is moved with compassion for us.

> For I perceive that ye desire that I should show unto you what I have done unto your brethren at Jerusalem, for I see that your faith is sufficient that I should heal you.
>
> And it came to pass that when he had thus spoken, all the multitude, with one accord, did go forth with their sick and their afflicted, and their lame, and with their blind, and with their dumb, and with all them that were afflicted in any manner; and he did heal them every one as they were brought forth unto him.
>
> And they did all, both they who had been healed and they who were whole, bow down at his feet, and did worship him; and as many as could come for the multitude did kiss his feet, insomuch that they did bathe his feet with their tears. (3 Nephi 17:8–10)

My own tears flow as I read that passage, and I yearn for a day when I too may kiss His feet.

We also witness during His visit to the Nephites, as we saw during His ministry in ancient Israel, His tender care for children. In this setting He is joined by angels to guard and to bless these precious ones as they receive His pure love:

> And he spake unto the multitude, and said unto them: Behold your little ones.
>
> And as they looked to behold they cast their eyes towards

heaven, and they saw the heavens open, and they saw angels descending out of heaven as it were in the midst of fire; and they came down and encircled those little ones about, and they were encircled about with fire; and the angels did minister unto them. (3 Nephi 17:23–24)

Perhaps the greatest testimony of His love in the account of His visit to those in the New World is reflected in His willingness to plead unto the Father in their behalf. Having already accomplished the work He alone could do to atone for and redeem us in Gethsemane and on the cross, and having been resurrected so that we would also live again after our time in mortality, yet He would and will still plead with the Father in our favor.

And no tongue can speak, neither can there be written by any man, neither can the hearts of men conceive so great and marvelous things as we both saw and heard Jesus speak; and no one can conceive of the joy which filled our souls at the time we heard him pray for us unto the Father. (3 Nephi 17:17)

And in our time, the Lord has revealed His pleas to His Father on our behalf:

Listen to him who is the advocate with the Father, who is pleading your cause before him—Saying: Father, behold the sufferings and death of him who did no sin, in whom thou wast well pleased; behold the blood of thy Son which was shed, the blood of him whom thou gavest that thyself might be glorified; Wherefore, Father, spare these my brethren that believe on my name, that they may come unto me and have everlasting life. (Doctrine and Covenants 45:3–5)

Have you ever closed your eyes and imagined what it would feel like to see and hear your Savior pray to His Father for you? Perhaps He would express gratitude for the desire of your heart to follow Him, for the gifts you bring, for your kindness to His children, for your patience in bearing up in challenging situations, for the other things that only He and you know about yourself. Imagine hearing Him plead that your faith will hold strong and continue to grow, that your ability to be His hands in the world will be enhanced, that your courage will not fail, that the challenges and worries only you and He know you bear will become sources of strength, that you will have everlasting life through your faith in Him. What would it feel like to see and hear Him express His love for His Father and for you?

Having absorbed these things, is there anything you would hold back from Him? Is there anything He could ask that you would not want to offer, and offer wholeheartedly? And then, could you imagine that you know any individual you would not wish to likewise experience this same overwhelming miracle of love? How would such an experience change your life, your focus, your gratitude, and your prayers?

Recalling the faithless servant who refused to deploy what his master had entrusted to him (see Matthew 25), we know that His gift of love to us is never meant to remain with us alone: "A new commandment I give unto you, That ye love one another; as I have loved you, that ye also love one another. By this shall all men know that ye are my disciples, if ye have love one to another" (John 13:34–35).

Like the gift of rain in the Arizona desert, His love is sent to change barren to verdant, nascent to mature, possibility to fulfilled measure of creation.

In this perfect and limitless virtuous circle, as we feel His love, as we come to more fully know His character, we desire to share it with our neighbors. And as we love our neighbors, as we see the effect in their lives of His goodness, as we are able to divine what He loves about them, our love for Him grows. Thus extends an upward spiral of deeper knowledge and increasing love for both neighbor and God.

As we grow in love for God and for all of His children, Christ finds joy in seeing us progress toward Him. I am convinced that He is pleased with every effort, even the tiny steps we take each day, to become more like Him. We feel His love confirming the validity of our attempts, even His gratitude for our desires to follow Him.

CHAPTER THREE

FOR THE SON OF MAN IS COME TO SAVE THAT WHICH IS LOST

When in disgrace with fortune and men's eyes
I all alone beweep my outcast state,
And trouble deaf heaven with my bootless cries,
And look upon myself, and curse my fate,
Wishing me like to one more rich in hope,
Featured like him, like him with friends possessed,
Desiring this man's art, and that man's scope,
With what I most enjoy contented least;
Yet in these thoughts my self almost despising,
Haply I think on thee, and then my state,
Like to the lark at break of day arising
From sullen earth, sings hymns at heaven's gate;
For thy sweet love remembered such wealth brings
That then I scorn to change my state with kings.

—William Shakespeare, *Sonnet 29*

Do you have a memory of losing something valuable? Maybe you've had the especially searing experience of temporarily losing a child, with emotions going from wonder to annoyance to concern to bone-deep fear within a few seconds. In that instant, did you abandon the format of prayer to plead with Heavenly Father, "Oh, please help me, please help me"?

We can rightly understand all of Jesus's ministry, all of His life, and indeed His foreordained role in the plan of happiness as a single-minded quest to save a lost child. In this case, the child could be considered as every person ever to be born in mortality. Without His atoning sacrifice and Resurrection, physical death is the end of every story, forever. Because of Him, all will live again, and the choice to return to the presence of our Heavenly Parents and Redeemer becomes ours to make, "for the power is in them" (Doctrine and Covenants 58:28).

In the superlative trio of parables that reaches its apex with the allegory of The Righteous Father of Two Sons, Jesus first provided two other examples of how the listeners of His time would have understood feeling impelled to search for lost things.

> What man of you, having an hundred sheep, if he lose one of them, doth not leave the ninety and nine in the wilderness, and go after that which is lost, until he find it? And when he hath found it, he layeth it on his shoulders, rejoicing. And when he cometh home, he calleth together his friends and neighbours, saying unto them, Rejoice with me; for I have found my sheep which was lost. . . .
>
> Either what woman having ten pieces of silver, if she lose one piece, doth not light a candle, and sweep the house, and seek diligently till she find it? And when she hath found it, she calleth her friends and her neighbours together, saying, Rejoice with me; for I have found the piece which I had lost. (Luke 15:4–6, 8–9)

Jesus uses these illustrations to highlight the joy in heaven over every repentant individual, salvation in its most crucial sense. As we look at the layers of meaning in parables, here, I believe, we also see illustrated the Savior's care for every situation of our lives that causes us to feel lost.

Sometimes we can feel lost because events in our lives are not proceeding as we had hoped or expected. Sister Kristen Oaks shared this experience:

> On one occasion, full of worry and frustration about my single situation and my advancing years, I went to a priesthood leader for a blessing to strengthen me. The words spoken in that blessing stay with me to this day and ring truer to me as time passes. I can still quote them: "If you cannot bear the difficulties and challenges of single life, you will never be able to bear the difficulties and challenges of married life." I sat a bit stunned. Those words were a call to action for me to make my life wonderful regardless of any situation or difficulty I faced. ("To the Singles of the Church," CES Devotional for Young Adults, September 11, 2011)

One source of deep pain can be lost trust. A dear friend and I spent many hours talking after she learned that her husband had carried on an extramarital affair with a work colleague for a period of months. During that time, he had told his wife a number of lies to hide what he was doing and how he was spending his time. As she tried to move forward at this bleak point in her life, she repeated the question over and over: "Can I ever trust him again?" Obviously, that trust, which had been lost in the instant when the truth came to light, could not be regained quickly. They began a process together of learning to communicate more openly and effectively. He took steps to demonstrate his determination to put his wife and family first in his life, part of a restitution effort in his process of seeking forgiveness. Over time, as they both prayerfully sought to restore what had been lost and focused on their covenantal relationship with God in their marriage, my friend found peace. She was able to regain confidence in her husband, and she found renewed trust through the Lord's care.

Putting yourself in the position of both wife and husband in this experience, can you recognize and feel that each had a loss—her trust, his self-worth—that was healed because they could access our Savior's love for them?

We live in a time of great discord in the world. Social media makes it easy to bully and demean. Instant publication of rumor or opinion as if it were factual information means that the accuracy of what we read has often been neither researched nor reviewed, and those with large numbers of followers may have disproportionate influence unrelated to expertise or integrity. A feeling of loss of inclusion caused by constant strife may be profound.

A respected friend, J. Stuart Adams, who serves as a state legislative leader in the United States, pointed me toward the dedicatory prayer of the Salt Lake Temple, offered by President Wilford Woodruff on April 6, 1893. After President Woodruff had issued a Manifesto in 1890 ending the official practice of polygamy, which was a condition for statehood, two political parties organized in the territory of Utah began actively preparing for statehood and federal elections. In the dedicatory prayer, President Woodruff said:

> O God, the Eternal Father, Thou knowest all things. Thou seest the course Thy people have been led to take in political

matters. They have, in many instances, joined the two great national parties. Campaigns have been entered upon, elections have been held, and much party feeling has been engendered. Many things have been said and done which have wounded the feelings of the humble and the meek, and which have been a cause of offense. We beseech Thee, in Thine infinite mercy and goodness, to forgive Thy people wherein they have sinned in this direction. Show them, O Father, their faults and their errors, that they may see the same in the light of Thy Holy Spirit, and repent truly and sincerely, and cultivate that spirit of affection and love which Thou art desirous that all the children of men should entertain one for another, and which Thy Saints, above all others, should cherish. Enable Thy people hereafter to avoid bitterness and strife, and to refrain from words and acts in political discussions that shall create feeling and grieve Thy Holy Spirit.

Although President Woodruff's plea was specific to the circumstances of that place and time, I am certain we can draw a larger lesson. In any of our interactions—in person, online, or through other media—we have an individual obligation to ensure that our words create feelings that are harmonious with the Holy Spirit. We are unlikely to suddenly agree with all around us in political matters, but we can disagree with special care for how our communications will be heard by the humble and meek.

We gain strength to act in this way—strength that our lives might fulfill President Woodruff's prayer, strength to be leaven in the loaf of public discourse, strength so that our efforts can be a balm to those who are otherwise buffeted by discord and disunity—when we seek the enabling power of Christ's Atonement, His loving gift of grace.

Another way we can invite the influence of the Lord's love into our lives is to follow His oft-repeated commandments to care for the poor and needy, to seek through Him a sense of nonjudgmental empathy and compassion that is largely lost in the world today. By revelation in February 1831, the Lord said: "If thou lovest me thou shalt serve me and keep all my commandments. And behold, thou wilt remember the poor, and consecrate of thy properties for their support" (Doctrine and Covenants 42:29–30). It seems to me that our Savior intends us to be actively engaged in rescuing the poor, not leaving them alone to find their own way to happier days. As President Marion G. Romney noted:

> There is an interdependence between those who have and those who have not. The process of giving exalts the poor and humbles the rich. In the process, both are sanctified. The poor, released from the bondage and limitations of poverty, are enabled as free men to rise to their full potential, both temporally and spiritually. The rich, by imparting of their surplus, participate in the eternal principle of giving. Once a person has been made whole or self-reliant, he reaches out to aid others, and the cycle repeats itself.
>
> We are all self-reliant in some areas and dependent in others. Therefore, each of us should strive to help others in areas where we have strengths. At the same time, pride should not prevent us from graciously accepting the helping hand of another when we have a real need. To do so denies another person

the opportunity to participate in a sanctifying experience. ("The Celestial Nature of Self-reliance," *Ensign*, November 1982)

As an organization, and in partnership with other churches and nongovernmental groups, The Church of Jesus Christ of Latter-day Saints does amazing work to aid and improve the lives of the poor around the world. In 2019, the Church provided humanitarian services in 142 countries and territories on 3,221 projects with more than 2,000 partners to serve millions of people. Since 1985, over $2.3 billion in assistance has been provided (see churchofjesuschrist.org). We can be justly proud and grateful for the work made possible by donations of money and professional skills by many Church members and friends. But it would still be profitable to ask ourselves some more personal questions: Have I lost my own desire to help the poor? Am I seeking to feel the Lord's love in my life and to share His love with all around me? What can I personally do, besides giving money, that will make a difference in someone's life?

May I share a couple of examples you might consider?

I have a wonderful friend, Steve Kenny, who is a convert to the Church. He is well educated, uses his professional skills and accreditation in a successful career, and is an active and converted Latter-day Saint. He is also a very humble person and one of the most genuinely kind men I know. He would be both surprised and embarrassed to be singled out for praise. Each Sunday afternoon, he spends hours in local jails and prisons as part of the Church's program to aid incarcerated individuals. He is sought out and appreciated by those with whom he works.

But my friend doesn't let his personal ministry end with his work in the Church's prisoner outreach program; he is attuned to need wherever he sees it. One Monday around lunchtime, he was asked for money to buy food by a young man on the street who looked as though he was in a bad way. Steve invited this young man, Donnie, to go into a restaurant with him so they could have lunch together. Donnie had several addictions, including to heroin, and because he had not been able to obtain the drug for a period, he was in unwanted withdrawal and could scarcely eat. In the course of the conversation, he indicated that his grandmother and other relatives were members of The Church of Jesus Christ of Latter-day Saints. Steve directed Donnie to a methadone clinic and invited him to come to the chapel later that evening. Steve said he would arrange for the bishop to be there, who would help Donnie in whatever way he could. As Steve and the bishop arrived at the chapel, they found Donnie lying on the sidewalk in front of the building. They helped him in, and the bishop introduced himself and stayed engaged with Donnie and Steve to provide help over time.

Donnie was eventually able to complete addiction recovery programs and has been clean from drugs and alcohol use for over three years. He holds down a steady job, has received promotions, and earns enough to live independently as well as to provide regular support for his daughter, with whom he has built a relationship after having been absent for five years. He has focused on getting a GED certificate and is planning to begin work on an associate's degree. He has been baptized and ordained to priesthood office and serves as building coordinator for his ward. Donnie says that having the keys to the chapel in his pocket represents more trust than he has ever before been shown. A conversation with Donnie is filled with enthusiasm, happiness, and gratitude. At each step of this wonderful and miraculous process, Steve has been a reliable source of support and encouragement. Isn't it wonderful how one person can help another change a life, and, in so doing, change the course of generations to come?

Why does Steve spend his time in this way, and why was Donnie able to make such a powerful change in his life? Both, feeling the love of Christ, have been impelled to restore losses: loss of freedom as a result of incarceration or addiction, loss of self-worth, as well as a lack of the spiritual gift of hope in Christ. Lives are healed, like ripples in a pond, as the impact of the Savior's love changes one life, then another, and another.

Earlier in my career, I became aware of an organization near my office that was looking for volunteers. The HOPE Program began in 1984 with a mission to help long-term unemployed people find jobs. There are many reasons why someone may be out of the workforce for a prolonged time, including addiction, incarceration, full-time care of children or parents, and serious illness. The organization recognized as impediments to getting and keeping a job not only the lack of direct skills and prior experience, but also the many social needs of this population. The program provided assistance in finding housing, food, and clothing. Individuals were required to be clean and sober before beginning the program. Each day for twelve weeks, program participants were required to be in class on time (to learn the skill of being reliable at work). They received training in personal computer skills as well as instruction and practice with common applications such as Word and Excel. They learned to manage personal finances and improve interpersonal skills, and they were armed with tools for conflict resolution. In the second half of their course, they were given internships with local companies so that they could have a current job and skill to build their resumés. I was able, with my colleagues, to implement mock interviews to teach the skills of best presenting oneself in a job interview.

Over a period of years, I had the opportunity to meet many participants in the HOPE Program, and each interaction left me with a profound feeling of respect for the courage and optimism of these individuals. Many overcame tremendously difficult challenges in their lives. I left every meeting with enormous gratitude for the gift each person had given me to be witness to their efforts, to see their willingness to be honest and open with a stranger and their trust that my colleagues and I genuinely wanted to support them. They saw the best in us as they allowed us to see it in them. The statistics were against them: at that time, the program had a 25 percent success rate, defined as an individual getting a job and remaining continuously employed for twenty-four months after the program, compared to the success rate of a comparable city-sponsored program at only 12 percent. I often marveled that these people would work so hard knowing how high the odds were against them. And yet, all of us felt such joy for each individual who did succeed—again, changing the course of generations.

You have felt the same way, I am certain, when you have had the opportunity to render service to a sister or brother in need. In those moments, we receive the gift of feeling God's love for that person—and for us. Even if it has been a while since you have acted as Christ's hands in this world, know that somewhere very nearby is someone whom He is eager to bless through your efforts. As you pray for the opportunity to serve, circumstances will arise for you to do so, and you will feel so grateful that the Lord would allow you to be the means of bringing His loving care to another.

The Church has played a lead role in creating JustServe.org, a website where the volunteer needs of organizations may be posted and volunteers may search for places to serve in their own area. You can find there many ways to invest your time and skills in helping those who are lost in one way or another.

It has been several years since the Church launched the "I Was a Stranger" initiative to assist members in their individual efforts to help refugees. The need has not lessened, and the opportunities to help have, if anything, only grown.

> Being a refugee may be a defining moment in the lives of those who are refugees, but being a refugee does not define *them.* Like countless thousands before them, this will be a period—we hope a short period—in their lives. Some of them will go on to be Nobel laureates, public servants, physicians, scientists, musicians, artists, religious leaders, and contributors in other fields. Indeed, many of them *were* these things before they lost everything. This moment does not define them, but our response will help define us. (Patrick Kearon, "Refuge from the Storm," *Ensign,* May 2016; emphasis in original)

JustServe.org and "I Was A Stranger" are both programs that reflect inspired responses by leaders who feel the love of Christ in their own lives and strive to exponentially increase the impact of that love throughout the world. And yet, the power of both efforts comes from a recognition that our response to the enormous needs of this world doesn't require a class or quorum to get involved. That power comes as our individual hearts are changed and each one of us reaches out to those around us to share the love we more powerfully feel from our Savior. Sharon Eubank, professionally the head of Latter-day Saint Charities and in her Church calling a member of the General

Relief Society Presidency, gave an enlightening address to students of Brigham Young University in which she observed:

> There are many, many organizations and people who do enormous amounts of good in the world with their limited resources and their Benjamin-like desires to serve their fellow beings and to serve God. I am privileged to work with many of them, and I get to see what is being done in the world. I am going to speak to you from my own experience now about what I have seen that accomplishes the most lasting good. If you want to be involved in humanitarian service, this is the way—and I hope this is the thing that you will remember from the forum today. *You are the gift.* You yourself are the gift. It is not the clothing, the hygiene kits, the school desks, or the wells. It is you.
>
> What would it look like if each of us were our own well-stocked humanitarian organization? Instead of just giving out tangible goods in foreign locations, what if we had the richness of dispensing healing, friendship, respect, peaceful dialogue, sincere interest, protective listening of children, birthday remembrances, and conversations with strangers? What if that was what your humanitarian organization did? This kind of humanitarian work can be done by anybody and it can be done at any time. And you don't need warehouses or fundraising or transportation. You can be perfectly responsive to any need that comes to you, wherever you are. ("Turning Enemies into Friends," Brigham Young University Forum, January 23, 2018; emphasis added)

Understand that "you are the gift." Even more than whatever tangible aid you can provide, it is your compassion and empathy, your awareness of individuals and willingness to see them, that will help the most. You are the gift because you have received the gift of Christ's love and are determined to share it. Your disposition to listen and to learn and your humble desire to share your love—these are the things that make a difference in others' lives and allow you to experience what Jesus was trying to convey:

> Then shall the righteous answer him, saying, Lord, when saw we thee an hungred, and fed thee? or thirsty, and gave thee drink? When saw we thee a stranger, and took thee in? or naked, and clothed thee? Or when saw we thee sick, or in prison, and came unto thee? And the King shall answer and say unto them, Verily I say unto you, Inasmuch as ye have done it unto one of the least of these my brethren, ye have done it unto me. (Matthew 25:37–40)

When we gain or regain a desire to help the lost, the poor, the refugee, the unemployed, the incarcerated, we find ourselves, our truest selves, among those who would be disciples of Jesus Christ. In those moments of service, we feel the Lord's love even more strongly and consistently than we ever have before.

Finally, another indication of the Lord's desire to restore what has been lost may occur when the routines of our church experience have caused us to treat as commonplace His gift of restored power.

To share one specific example, I had the wonderful privilege of teaching a weekly study group for a nearby mid-singles ward on the New Testament. We studied the same scripture block each week as the *Come, Follow Me* course, and we considered in-depth some of the topics most meaningful to ward members. The four Gospels provided the inestimable gift of allowing us to feel ourselves among the followers of Jesus, listening to His teachings, searching for the layers of meaning in His parables, and witnessing His miraculous power to heal, to bless, and to sanctify.

Each week, as I prepared, studied, pondered, and prayed in order to create a lesson, I realized again the accuracy of the saying that it is the teacher who learns the most. Questions would come to my mind as I read, which would prompt me toward further research and meditation. I tried to place myself in the position of the disciples, of the tax collectors, the centurions, the Sadducees and Pharisees, the wounded, the women. All would likely witness His ministry through the lens of their own life experiences, reflecting their own faith and hope. I searched for topics that would have the most meaning for class members, and for insights that could ignite and enliven their own study and prayers. Reading the footnotes of the excellent study Bible *The New Testament: A Translation for Latter-day Saints,* by Thomas A. Wayment, provided a further layer of comprehension, with cultural references, the prophecies known to contemporary witnesses, the inspired emendation by Joseph Smith, and comparisons between early source documents. Only a portion of the ideas, impressions, and insights I gained in my own study could form the basis for an hour of teaching and discussion. No wonder, then, that the teacher is likely to have gained the most learning! Hopefully, of course, the lesson and discussion will inspire those who attend to undertake their own further explorations of a given topic.

What is gospel teaching if not a means of transmitting Christ's love more broadly?

I am grateful for this experience, which has expanded my

appreciation for inspired actions by prophets and apostles that have such direct and beneficial impact in my life. I am thankful to witness the blessings of the *Come, Follow Me* method of gospel study in so many individuals and families around me. I marvel at the wisdom of "home-centered, Church-supported" learning: the role of teacher can be alternated among members of the family or group. This way, each person, rather than always being in the learner role, is also periodically gaining the advantage of the process that comes with learning in order to teach. This style of learning also allows parents to impart the messages that are most meaningful in that moment to their family members, to share their understanding of doctrines, their insights gained from personal revelation, and their experiences seeing the truths of the gospel affect the lives of others. Since parents are in the foremost position to know what methods of learning will be the most engaging to each child, they can organize lessons using elements that will reach each individual specifically. If a child is wrestling with a particular issue or challenge, the tuition of Christ's gospel can be tailored in tone, delivered with meekness and love unfeigned, to meet the needs of that child in that moment.

The experience of having no congregational services at church during the COVID-19 epidemic made even more essential the practices and skills developed in learning to become home-centered and Church-supported. Many extended families used the opportunity not only to strengthen family ties but also to deepen the conversion of each member. Some singles found use of social media and tools found on the internet to be essential links to others, filling crucial needs for interaction as well as spiritual growth. Some who had stepped away from Church activity before the pandemic rediscovered a community of Saints who had not forgotten them, and who ensured their physical and social needs were met. We also found some holes in our nets; we learned that we needed to be more creative and work more diligently to reach those whose circumstances rendered face-to-face ministry unavailable. I am grateful for those who reached out to me during this time, my family and ward members, neighbors and friends, to ensure that I was aware of their interest in me and in my well-being.

Perhaps we see more clearly during times of stress that the Savior's efforts to save what has been lost never wane. In whatever times and ways we are reminded, we understand more deeply that it is always His love, demonstrated through His atoning sacrifice and Resurrection, reflected in His constant care and awareness, that calls the wanderer home.

CHAPTER FOUR

HE GAVE HIS LIFE FOR HIS FRIENDS

This is my commandment,
That ye love one another, as I have loved you.
Greater love hath no man than this,
that a man lay down his life for his friends.
Ye are my friends, if ye do whatsoever I command you.
Henceforth I call you not servants;
for the servant knoweth not what his lord doeth:
but I have called you friends;
for all things that I have heard of my Father
I have made known unto you.

—John 15:12–15

For one who has spent his career in global banking, as I have, the concept of saving by giving away is not an obvious one to grasp! It is the paradox of faith: His death made possible our rebirth. It is also the paradox of friendship: we clearly realize deepened feelings for the One who has given us everything, and yet it is He who calls us friends.

Do you recall Jesus's parable of the Two Debtors?

And, behold, a woman in the city, which was a sinner, when she knew that Jesus sat at meat in the Pharisee's house, brought an alabaster box of ointment, and stood at his feet behind him weeping, and began to wash his feet with tears, and did wipe them with the hairs of her head, and kissed his feet, and anointed them with the ointment.

Now when the Pharisee which had bidden him saw it, he spake within himself, saying, This man, if he were a prophet, would have known who and what manner of woman this is that toucheth him: for she is a sinner.

And Jesus answering said unto him, Simon, I have somewhat to say unto thee. And he saith, Master, say on. There was a certain creditor which had two debtors: the one owed five hundred pence, and the other fifty. And when they had nothing to pay, he frankly forgave them both. Tell me therefore, which of them will love him most?

Simon answered and said, I suppose that he, to whom he forgave most. And he said unto him, Thou hast rightly judged. (Luke 7:37–43)

To know what we need to repent of, and to know that our repentance has been met with forgiveness, both seem to me to be matters of personal revelation. My experience is that my awareness of the Savior's love for me often comes in those moments when my love for Him has expanded because I am a beneficiary of His Atonement. I know that I am His friend because I have made use of His gift, freely offered.

Some things have to be experienced to be deeply and fully understood. Do you know what it feels like to have been so cold that putting your fingers or toes into tepid water creates a sensation like dipping into lava? Have you ever needed to use an oven mitt to avoid getting seriously burned when opening the door of a car that has been sitting in the desert sun? Only when you have had these experiences do they truly become real to you. Similarly, to fully absorb the love inherent in the gift of Christ's Atonement, we have to use it, to experience it for ourselves. And when we do, we know what it means to be His friend.

Like me, you probably remember how you felt when Elder Jeffrey R. Holland related the experience of two brothers scaling a canyon wall without climbing equipment, and the climactic moment when the older brother is unable to make the last distance to safety:

"Giving him enough time to be out of sight, I said my last prayer—that I wanted my family to know I loved them and that Jimmy could make it home safely on his own—then I leapt. There was enough adrenaline in my spring that the jump extended my arms above the ledge almost to my elbows. But as I slapped my hands down on the surface, I felt nothing but loose sand on flat stone. I can still remember the gritty sensation of hanging there with nothing to hold on to—no lip, no ridge, nothing to grab or grasp. I felt my fingers begin to recede slowly over the sandy surface. I knew my life was over.

"But then suddenly, like a lightning strike in a summer storm, two hands shot out from somewhere above the edge of the cliff, grabbing my wrists with a strength and determination that belied their size. My faithful little brother had not gone looking for any fictitious tree branch. Guessing exactly what I was planning to do, he had never moved an inch. He had simply waited—silently, almost breathlessly—knowing full well I would be foolish enough to try to make that jump. When I did, he grabbed me, held me, and refused to let me fall. Those strong brotherly arms saved my life that day as I dangled helplessly above what would surely have been certain death." ("Where Justice, Love, and Mercy Meet," *Ensign*, May 2015)

A friend, our Brother, does for us what we cannot do for ourselves in our moment of greatest need.

Reading the four Gospels, I have thought about how the original Apostles might have understood what Jesus was trying to teach them about His upcoming death and Resurrection. They were aware, from their scriptures, that Elijah had been the agent to return the widow's son to life, and that Elisha had raised the son of the Shunammite (see 1 Kings 17; 2 Kings 4). They had witnessed Jesus restore life to the daughter of Jairus, who had apparently died a short while earlier; they saw Him command the son of a widow in the town of Nain to arise, when he had been dead long enough to be on a funeral bier on the way to burial; and they saw Him raise Lazarus four days after his burial (see Mark 5:35–43; Luke 7:12–16; John 11:38–45). So these Apostles would have known of Jesus and His prophets bringing those who had died of natural causes back to life—they had seen Him cure disease in the living and in the dead. They had some experience seeing the dead brought back to life at Jesus's command. But what would they have understood of resurrection, of joining spirit with a perfected body? How could they have imagined Jesus's death from scourging and on the cross, His burial in the tomb of Joseph of Arimathea, and His time with them again afterward? Indeed, when they first learned of His Resurrection, as Luke records, "their words seemed to them as idle tales, and they believed them not" (Luke 24:11).

Jesus had taught of the love represented by His atoning sacrifice, which made it possible for us and all of our brothers and sisters— throughout the ages and in worlds without number—to be justified of errors and receive the strength to become sanctified. Now the Apostles would learn of His love expressed in His Resurrection, which enabled universal salvation from physical death. In the words of Elder D. Todd Christofferson:

> Consider for a moment the significance of the Resurrection in resolving once and for all the true identity of Jesus of Nazareth and the great philosophical contests and questions of life. If Jesus was in fact literally resurrected, it necessarily follows that He is a divine being. No mere mortal has the power in himself to come to life again after dying. Because He was resurrected, Jesus cannot have been only a carpenter, a teacher, a rabbi, or a prophet. Because He was resurrected, Jesus had to have been a God, even the Only Begotten Son of the Father.
>
> Therefore, what He taught is true; God cannot lie.
>
> Therefore, He was the Creator of the earth, as He said.
>
> Therefore, heaven and hell are real, as He taught.
>
> Therefore, there is a world of spirits, which He visited after His death.
>
> Therefore, He will come again, as the angels said, and "reign personally upon the earth."
>
> Therefore, there is a resurrection and a final judgment for all.
>
> Given the reality of the Resurrection of Christ, doubts about the omnipotence, omniscience, and benevolence of God the Father—who gave His Only Begotten Son for the redemption of the world—are groundless. Doubts about the meaning and purpose of life are unfounded. Jesus Christ is in fact the only name or way by which salvation can come to mankind. The grace of Christ is real, affording both forgiveness and

cleansing to the repentant sinner. ("The Resurrection of Jesus Christ," *Ensign*, May 2014)

Each week we are privileged to participate in the ordinance of the sacrament of the Lord's Supper. "As we sincerely listen to the sacrament prayers, phrases such as 'always remember him,' 'keep his commandments,' 'have his Spirit to be with them' will fill our hearts with an overwhelming desire to be better. Then when we partake of the bread and the water with a broken heart and a contrite spirit, I know we can feel and even hear those most wondrous words, 'I love you. I love you'" (John H. Groberg, "The Power of God's Love," *Ensign*, November 2004).

He is our friend, and "we love him, because he first loved us" (1 John 4:19). He is our friend because of His sacrifice in our behalf. With His stripes we are healed, and we are graven upon the palms of His hands (see Isaiah 53:5; 49:16).

His offering was made for His friends, those He loves without end, you and me. Can our actions make us better friends to Him? The book of Proverbs gives us an idea: "A friend loveth at all times, and a brother is born for adversity" (Proverbs 17:17).

I was invited to lunch by a friend who wanted to introduce me to another friend, a man who had previously served as a mission president. This man had questions about how best to support elders and sisters from his mission who, during or after their missionary service, had shared with him that they were gay, lesbian, bisexual, transgender, intersex, asexual, or queer. As we talked about his missionaries, he asked about my life. At one point, he asked a question that startled me: "Do you think the Lord loves you as much as He does your brother?"

Often when people I've just met ask something about "your

brother," I make a point of saying that I have four brothers—about which one are they curious? I know quite well which brother they mean—Elder Christofferson—but I feel a fierce loyalty to all of my brothers and don't want any of the other three, less well-known ones to feel slighted, even when they aren't present!

On this occasion, I didn't banter about which brother. My thoughts immediately went to my lifetime of experience with the love of my earthly parents and family, and to my personal feelings of God's knowledge of and care for me. The very question seemed to me off base. Regaining equilibrium, I answered that I was certain God loved my brother and me equally because He loves all of His children unqualifiedly. I said, though, that I believed our Heavenly Father has loved my brother's obedience more than my own, and I felt my brother had earned His trust.

As I think now about that lunchtime conversation, I would add that I feel my brother and others whose lives reflect their devotion to Him have become Christ's steadfast and consistent friends, in the way we read in the Doctrine and Covenants. By revelation, the Lord provides His own perspective: "And again I say unto you, my friends, for from henceforth I shall call you friends, it is expedient that I give unto you this commandment, that ye become even as my friends in days when I was with them, traveling to preach the gospel in my power" (Doctrine and Covenants 84:77).

All of us, not solely those called to positions of significant responsibility in the Church, become His more dependable friends as we strive, together with Him, to serve and gather His children on both sides of the veil.

I had a conversation some time ago with a former bishop and

later stake president of Young Single Adult units, as I was preparing to speak at a YSA fireside. He said, "The most important thing you can tell them is that they should find out that the Lord loves them." The insight this man had gained through his years of service to young adults was that when we feel known and loved individually by the Lord, our natural reaction is to reach outward, to share that love with those around us. As we thus act on both the first and second great commandments, we become our Savior's fellow servants and His friends.

Since that time, I have had the opportunity to teach institute classes, seminary classes, and the single adult study group mentioned earlier, and with each interaction I have come to understand more deeply the wisdom of that leader's comment—and not just for young adults. Each of us needs to know that we are known and seen by the Lord. For some there will come a moment of such acute distress that a plea to God, "Do You know me?," is the only possible action. I had such an experience as part of my coming-out process. The feeling of not belonging anywhere, not really fitting into any group, was powerful, and I feared this would be my lot throughout life. In that moment, at the very early stage of trying to understand what it meant in my life to be gay, I felt that a failed marriage and enormous unhappiness had proven that I could not fully be included as a Latter-day Saint. But my values and goals in life, together with my feeling that I was insufficiently physically attractive, seemed to mean that I would never fully fit as a gay man. Offering that four-word prayer seemed like the end of the road, and yet the immediate feeling of warmth and energy reassured me that I was known, I was a person of value, and there was always Someone who beckoned to me. In that sense, it was the beginning of a new road.

Some may question why the Lord would answer my prayer when I was not primarily seeking a path of repentance; indeed, I had already asked to be excommunicated from His Church. Do you think the supposition behind that question is that we have to be worthy for our prayers to be answered? Instinctively we know that is not the case. Our worth as children of Heavenly Parents is eternal and unchanging. Our righteousness is never perfect. Imperfect as I was and am, I knew that what I felt was real, and it left me in no doubt as to the source of the response.

Virginia Hinckley Pearce shared an experience she had been told by the young man in this story:

> When he was about fifteen, going to church seemed to have less and less relevance to his life. And when he got a part-time job that often included a Sunday shift, it became even easier to miss meetings. Within about a year he had drifted into a morally difficult lifestyle and was unhappy and discouraged. He had difficulty sleeping and would often walk the streets in the earliest hours of the day. He told me he was doing just that at about 3 a.m. one morning when something happened. He said that it was sudden. He felt God's love surround him. He went home and got out his scriptures and began reading. Over a period of several months he basked and grew, fed by the influence of the Spirit. His life changed. He repented and returned to church. This boy's story may seem odd, even unfair when we read that we are required to keep the commandments in order to feel the Spirit, but God, in His infinite wisdom, knows how and when

to succor us with His love. It is His to give and ours to accept in gratitude. It is part of the glorious and infinite gift of the Atonement. (*A Heart Like His: Making Space for God's Love in Your Life* [2016], 31–32)

The gratitude we feel for those moments of transcendent love is a powerful impetus to make certain those around us also bask in His warmth and succor. In such times, we are reminded that we are always His children and His care is unceasing. We can act on the desire we feel that this love is too profound *not* to share, and thus engage on the course of working alongside Him as His friends who are also His servants. I think of the words in our hymnal, whose author is unknown:

> *He'll call, persuade, direct aright,*
> *And bless with wisdom, love, and light,*
> *In nameless ways be good and kind,*
> *But never force the human mind.*
> ("Know This, That Every Soul Is Free," *Hymns,* no. 240)

We can be hesitant to call on Him when we feel unworthy (as if we could ever truly *merit* His companionship in this life). I believe the feeling that we should not ask for His love and notice does not come from Him, but rather from a source designed to keep us away from His care. I have talked to a number of people over the years about their experience when asking God if He knows them, and my conclusion is that this is a prayer He delights to answer. We don't approach it as if we are seeking a sign, but rather with the clarity of a heartfelt need to have something to hold onto. Even if the prayer is not answered immediately, it seems to allow the Lord to do something in His own time that I believe is for Him a pleasure: to show His love.

When we receive our uniquely individual answer to such a prayer, it can be the basis of increased faith, hope, and charity. Feeling His love fills us with a desire, like Lehi experiencing the fruit of the tree in his vision, to share it with everyone around us. As we do, we are not only recipients of the superlative gift that has made Him our friend, our changed hearts help us become His friends who toil together with Him that all may come and feel, come and stay.

PART TWO

OUR LOVE FOR CHRIST

CHAPTER FIVE

KNOWING THE LORD
WE WORSHIP

We prize kindness, we value tenderness, and we esteem compassion.
Who can doubt the most transcendent instance of human love is a testament
to a more perfect source, a love without limit?
We are continuing, with tragic and devastating exceptions,
on the trajectory inaugurated by Adam and Eve,
becoming ever more like God,
as we become ever more adept at discerning good and evil,
and nourishing the wellsprings of human love.
And in so doing, we grow more capable of discerning
a kind and merciful God among His many counterfeits.

— Terryl Givens and Fiona Givens, *The God Who Weeps:*
How Mormonism Makes Sense of Life (2012), 20

Perhaps you have had an experience similar to mine. Growing up, I felt there was something about me that the Lord needed to change, so I fasted, prayed, pleaded, and tried to obey my way into perfect worthiness. Somehow, I had transformed the promise, "I, the Lord, am bound when ye do what I say" (Doctrine and Covenants 82:10), into a sense that my righteousness could obligate Heavenly Father to do what I asked in the manner and timing that I wanted. Stated in those terms, the idea is appalling: gaining virtue for the purpose of manipulating God.

We understand the scriptural promises made to those who seek Him and follow His commandments. We also realize that this life is intended to be a time of learning to act in faith, through periods of plenty as much as in seasons of scarcity. How can we harmonize those two understandings?

And although we know that there are moments to "Be still, and know that I am God" (Psalm 46:10), clearly the Lord does not intend that we should be passive, waiting to be acted upon. For we have also the compelling command that women and men "should be anxiously engaged in a good cause, and do many things of their own free will, and bring to pass much righteousness; *For the power is in them,* wherein they are agents unto themselves. And inasmuch as men do good they shall in nowise lose their reward. But he that doeth not anything until he is commanded, and receiveth a commandment with doubtful heart, and keepeth it with slothfulness, the same is damned" (Doctrine and Covenants 58:27–29, emphasis added).

How can we know when and how to act, and when to wait upon the Lord?

In my experience, the answers to these questions begin to come as we seek to know Him. Scriptures are a helpful beginning, and hearing the testimonies of those who are called as His special witnesses often provides additional clarity. But it is in our interactions with Him— through praying in His name, through serving our brothers and sisters—that we truly come to know Him.

As we seek Him, though, how can we avoid the subtle trap of attempting to turn the Lord into a creation in *our* own image, one whose responses are under our control, even as we proclaim Him omnipotent? The answer, I believe, is through an unsparing, critical, and honest examination of our motives. We need to recognize how our desires affect the lives of others and to engage in the ongoing process of working to align our will with His. May I share with you some of the learning I have gained through the choices I have made, and by watching the impact of decisions made by others?

THE MOTIVATION OF PRIDE

As the youngest of five sons in a family that loved and lived the gospel of Jesus Christ, when I distanced myself from the Church as a young man, I felt a need to prove that I was still a person of worth. In an era when being openly gay was still treated as disagreeable in many settings, even though I felt acceptance and love from my family, I harbored a sense that since I wasn't meeting cultural stereotypes of what it meant to be a "good son," I therefore needed to outperform in other areas. In a positive way, that meant that I made an early determination to hold onto every good thing from my upbringing, to actively seek to do good in the world, to make my corner of it a better place. I resolved that I would be a moral person, one who was kind-hearted and could be trusted.

But my need to manifest worthiness had a negative aspect as well. I felt I had to be visibly successful in my career, especially in a financial sense. I was grateful that I had a vocation that was both intellectually and geographically interesting to me, and the monetary rewards for achievement were generous. In their later years, my parents suffered some financial reverses, and I was delighted to do what I could to help. In some ways, I felt like helping them was a sort of "in-kind" tithing, a benefaction for the opportunities that I had been given. If

I'm completely candid about it, though, at some level I also felt that helping them made me more acceptable in their community. I placed value on the trappings of affluence and was willing for my financial contributions to great causes and organizations to be "seen of men." In a sense, I was wrapping a protective cloak around myself. The slings and arrows aimed by others at both the reality of my life and the choices I had made couldn't harm me if I projected a favorable image of being more financially successful than many who might be critical of me. Yet, in a sense, some of that generosity to others came from a place of shortage (fear of the opinion of others) rather than of abundance (acting solely from feelings of love).

That is how I learned the lesson of how our purposes are absorbed into our actions. It is not an easy thing to do, to honestly interrogate ourselves about our core motivations. Our usual practice is to look "on the outward appearance, but the Lord looketh on the heart" (1 Samuel 16:7), so we need to seek His help, even in understanding our own desires. I have found that, just as with my need to be seen as financially successful, pride is often the driver behind my requests to God. I hope I am making progress in my desire to shift from seeking the approval of others, even those I love, to making the Lord the sole guiding light of my life. "Submission to God, among many things, requires us to strip ourselves of our pride in order to be obedient to Him. In that process we make ourselves so much more useful in the achievement of God's purposes among His children," noted Elder Neal A. Maxwell (*Not My Will, but Thine* [1988, 2008], 94).

Paul, in his letter to Timothy, observes that the love of money is at evil's heart (see 1 Timothy 6:10). Jacob suggests that there can be a righteous purpose associated with seeking wealth: "And after ye have obtained a hope in Christ ye shall obtain riches, if ye seek them; and ye will seek them for the intent to do good—to clothe the naked, and to feed the hungry, and to liberate the captive, and administer relief to the sick and the afflicted" (Jacob 2:19). Hyrum Smith was given an individual charge: "Seek not for riches but for wisdom; and, behold, the mysteries of God shall be unfolded unto you, and then shall you be made rich. Behold, he that hath eternal life is rich" (Doctrine and Covenants 11:7). Many good people are adherents of prosperity theology, believing that financial well-being and physical health are always God's will for them. It is true that Alma invites us: "Cry unto him over the crops of your fields, that ye may prosper in them. Cry over the flocks of your fields, that they may increase" (Alma 34:24–25). But Moroni cautions us, "For behold, ye do love money, and your substance, and your fine apparel, and the adorning of your churches, more than ye love the poor and the needy, the sick and the afflicted" (Mormon 8:37). If we have somehow gained the impression that the mark of righteousness is ease and comfort, we ought to ask ourselves what of Peter, what of James, what of Paul? As great disciples and Apostles, with the power to bring the dead to life, did they enjoy a carefree life—repeatedly being thrown into prison, crucified (Peter), clubbed and stoned to death (James), or beheaded (Paul)? Are we greater than they, that the Lord should make rough places smooth for us? In fact, for those who are urgently following Christ, are not public derision and scorn more frequently occurring experiences than widespread acclaim and respect?

As I consider the experiences of the original disciples of Christ, the early Latter-day Saints, and modern Christians living in communities and countries hostile to their beliefs, I wonder, is it realistic to expect that our lives in the Church should always be glossy and easy?

I love the maxim that the gospel is intended to comfort the afflicted and afflict the comfortable! In that vein, isn't a regular reflection on our level of conversion, on our actions in support of our beliefs, on how well we are keeping the first and second great commandments, always going to elicit some internal discomfort and discontent?

God's gifts to an individual may include the ability to gain the blessing and trial of riches, but we err if we conflate righteousness with affluence. When Jesus teaches love for enemies, He says that it is required in order "that ye may be the children of your Father which is in heaven: for he maketh his sun to rise on the evil and on the good, and sendeth rain on the just and on the unjust" (Matthew 5:45). Presumably it is equally true that hurricanes and droughts also affect both commandment followers and commandment breakers. Therefore, neither poverty nor prosperity is an accurate indicator of an individual's fidelity to God.

The degree of ease I have in my life would have been inconceivable to those two or three generations before me, and I imagine they would have found it presumptuous in the extreme that I might ask God for more. As I continue to engage in this particular wrestle, some of the questions I ask myself are whether the financial or other blessings I seek are a distraction from my focus on knowing Christ, if my request stems from a desire to differentiate myself from others, how what I seek would advance His kingdom on earth in ways aligned with the talents and spiritual gifts I have been given, and whether I am authentically rather than conveniently looking "to the poor and the needy, and administer[ing] to their relief that they shall not suffer" (Doctrine and Covenants 38:35).

President Russell M. Nelson's social media post in June 2020 included this charge: "It behooves each of us to do whatever we can in our spheres of influence to preserve the dignity and respect every son and daughter of God deserves. . . . And we need to work tirelessly to build bridges of understanding rather than creating walls of segregation. I plead with us to work together for peace, for mutual respect and for an outpouring of love for all of God's children" (Tad Walch, "President Nelson: 'Deeply saddened at recent evidences of racism and a blatant disregard for human life,'" *Deseret News*, June 1, 2020).

Are we casting our net of burden sharing wide enough? We hope that church is a place where we feel close to Christ and experience His love, in the presence of His Holy Spirit. And yet, when we know that people with whom we worship are silently dealing with serious challenges, and that they may well be feeling that they don't fit and don't belong, shouldn't it make us squirm to realize that we are not bearing their burdens because they haven't trusted us enough to share them? And if and when they do trust us, might we not reasonably expect that sharing that load will cause us to groan, and perhaps even to challenge our perceptions of the world as a result? Such a shift in perspective might become a valuable check to our pride.

THE MOTIVATION OF POWER OR INFLUENCE

Our motivations may also include the desire for positions of influence or authority, in business, politics, or the Church. "Whosoever will be great among you, let him be your minister; And whosoever will be chief among you, let him be your servant: Even as the Son of man came not to be ministered unto, but to minister, and to give his life a ransom for many" (Matthew 20:26–28). As I have worked with some singularly successful men and women in business, I have noticed that they generally pay attention to sometimes-invisible people—those who clean, those who serve meals, those who maintain buildings or provide security. These executives may subscribe to a Christian concept of servant-leadership, or they may simply have come to recognize the critical contributions made by those who are seldom seen and rarely praised.

The chairman of a large global investment bank, regularly listed among the 100 Most Influential People in the World, has observed on more than one occasion that there are many people in the world as smart as or smarter than he is, many who work as hard or harder, and therefore a big factor in his success is luck: the luck of knowing the right people, of being given a leg up at just the right moment, of being handed a visible assignment that dovetails well with his skills, of being in the right place when opportunities come up. I have appreciated his humility and willingness to acknowledge reality. It is so easy to believe that all the good things we enjoy are the result of our own efforts, intellect, and talents, and to forget the other important factors that played in our favor, factors that many others do not enjoy.

I had a wonderful experience serving on the advisory board of a well-rated business school. One of my favorite programs in that school was designed to support young men and women who were the first in their families to attend college. The leaders who had developed this program recognized that providing financial scholarships was just the first area of need—and the easiest one to fill. Perhaps of more meaningful impact was assisting these students in their high school years with preparing to apply to colleges; they usually didn't have anyone close to them who knew how to navigate these processes, and even sometimes didn't know anyone who would encourage them to do so. Once they were admitted, they needed additional support to learn how to learn at the collegiate level. They needed mentors whom they could call when the going got tough, when they were homesick or felt they were floundering among their classmates. Those mentors were great heroes: their personal time commitment and genuine interest made all the difference in many individuals' ability to learn how to succeed. The job placement process was often another area where these students needed some extra help. Their parents didn't have a network of friends who could help them get that all-important first job. They didn't have resources to identify which companies were growing, and which were more likely to have programs to help new employees move rapidly up the necessary learning curve.

Coming to know some of these remarkable young people gave me greater appreciation for the advantages I have enjoyed, and a determination never to fit my father's description of "a self-made man who worships his creator," his favorite dismissive categorization of one who refuses to acknowledge all the ways he has been helped by others. (My twenty-first-century translation of that saying is: "If the airport had a humility detector, he needn't worry about being delayed for a secondary screening.")

Have you ever tried to picture in your mind the scene as the Savior prepared to wash the feet of His Apostles, His friends? Having experienced the heat and humidity of the Holy Land, I find it easy to imagine how off-putting feet clad only in sandals would be after a long day's journey. Peter likewise was initially incredulous that his Master would perform such a lowly task for him, and Jesus responded, "If I wash thee not, thou hast no part with me" (John 13:8). I think those words of Christ provide insight into His statement, "The servant is not greater than his lord; neither he that is sent greater than he that sent him" (John 13:16). Our charge is to recognize that those we lead must have claim on our attention and care if both we and they are to succeed. They must know that our desires are for their growth and happiness; they must be the recipients of time, effort, and energy we invest for their benefit more directly than our own. This implies a sacrifice on our part to truly know them and to act in their best interests.

As you think about the Last Supper, consider all that Jesus knew lay ahead. Think about His devotional act of doing something that in the disciples' previous experience would have been performed only by the lowest-ranking servant. Can you imagine that His actions were in any way meant to advance His own interests? Did He do it for any reason other than to show His love for His disciples and to demonstrate one way they would manifest their care for others?

I am touched by the choice Pope Francis has made to travel to a prison in Rome each year of his papacy on Holy Thursday to celebrate the mass of the Lord's Supper, beginning by washing the feet of a number of the prisoners. In his remarks to these men, he has thanked them for their warm welcome to him. I find it a great reminder of the humble and sincere gratitude I hope I always feel when others allow me the privilege of serving them.

THE MOTIVATION OF FEAR

Another, and particularly unhelpful, motivation can be fear.

Let me begin by clearly stating what I am *not* talking about, which is mental illness. According to the National Institute of Mental Health, 31.1 percent of adults in the United States experience anxiety disorder at some point in their lives, and the lifetime prevalence of any anxiety disorder among adolescents is 31.9 percent. Depression is one of the most common mental disorders in the US (see National Institute of Mental Health, nimh.nih.gov). Causes and means of managing such challenges are individual, and self-care, as well as the assistance of competent physicians and therapists, is essential. Jane Clayson Johnson's book *Silent Souls Weeping: Depression—Sharing Stories, Finding Hope* is an excellent resource to increase our understanding of and compassion for serious and enormously challenging diseases. In this book, Johnson includes the spiritual impacts of mental disorder, the feeling so many experience that the heavens are closed to them. She reports: "The happy news is that, without exception, every person I interviewed *had* forged ahead and learned to maneuver through subsequent depressive episodes, knowing that feeling the loss of the Spirit is a symptom of the disease, not reality and certainly not a permanent condition. . . . Their stories don't offer a *cure* for depression, but they do provide a reassuring sampling of how a depressed person can press on when the circuits in the brain are preventing the Spirit of the Lord from flowing freely" (*Silent Souls Weeping* [2018], 20–21).

Even when we are emotionally and mentally healthy, though, we can perceive the Lord who gave us the ultimate gift—salvation and the opportunity for exaltation—as an impartial but perfectly precise scorekeeper. Perhaps this misunderstanding comes from scriptures referring to such things as "the righteous judgment of God; who will render to every man according to his deeds" (Romans 2:5–6). In line with principles taught by President Dallin H. Oaks, perhaps in the beloved hymn "I Am a Child of God," the lyrics that in my youth were changed from "all that I must *know*" to "all that I must *do*" could now be updated with something that speaks of who, as children of Heavenly Parents, we strive to *become* in order to live with Them again someday.

In contrast to the institutions of the world, which teach us to *know* something, the gospel of Jesus Christ challenges us to *become* something. Many Bible and modern scriptures speak of a final judgment at which all persons will be rewarded according to their deeds or works or the desires of their hearts. But other scriptures enlarge upon this by referring to our being judged by the *condition* we have achieved. The prophet Nephi describes the Final Judgment in terms of what we *have become*. . . .

Like other parables, this one [Laborers in the Vineyard] can teach several different and valuable principles. For present purposes its lesson is that the Master's reward in the Final Judgment will not be based on how long we have labored in the vineyard. We do not obtain our heavenly reward by punching a time clock. What is essential is that our labors in the workplace of the Lord have caused us to *become* something. For some of us, this requires a longer time than for others. . . .

Instead of being judgmental about others, we should be concerned about ourselves. We must not give up hope. We must not stop striving. We are children of God, and it is possible for us to become what our Heavenly Father would have us become. (Dallin H. Oaks, "The Challenge to Become," *Ensign*, November 2000; emphasis in original)

Ought this not help us more clearly understand Christ as One who lovingly draws us closer, helps us improve our desires, and teaches us to see the divine in others? It was He who identified the first and second great commandments and then said, "On these two commandments hang all the law and the prophets" (Matthew 22:40). He taught that love for His Father and for all the Father's children is the reason behind, and the purpose for, every law, commandment, and prophetic precept. He not only commands us to love, He shows us how to do so and thereby grants us renewed hearts. Of what, then, can we be afraid?

At one point in my career, I worked for a man who was a graduate of the US Merchant Marine Academy. He sincerely believed that people perform best when they experience fear that they are likely to fail; he thought such fear kept individuals working right at the peak of their capabilities. During my early years of working for him, the migraine headaches that I had previously experienced once every two or three years now came two or three times a week. For me, working on the knife-edge of fear was nearly debilitating. Clearly, each of us responds to this approach in different ways, and yet, I couldn't help drawing a parallel to the spiritual experience of mortality. The plan for us to do a perilous thing—to live in a world where we would no longer see our Father and where we were guaranteed to make poor choices and act contrary to His will—that plan also included Jesus's willingness to act as our Savior and Redeemer. He would feel every sorrow, pain, and affliction, and His gifts to each of us would be justification, sanctification, and resurrection, as well as the possibility for us to choose exaltation. He would make available to us His Spirit of comfort and guidance; we need not be alone, and no failure need stand forever.

We do not worship a God who says, "You're on your own, and if you succeed I will reward you, and if you fail I will punish you." The Father and Savior we worship promise, "We will be with you, we will to you where you are, we will bear you up, and if you choose to follow us, we will provide a means such that mistakes will become tools of learning. Our work and glory will be to help you live again with us and to live the quality of life that we do: eternal life."

"Fear rarely has the power to change our hearts, and it will never transform us into people who love what is right and who want to obey Heavenly Father," said Elder Dieter F. Uchtdorf, "People who are fearful may *say* and do the right things, but they do not *feel* the right things. They often feel helpless and resentful, even angry. Over time these feelings lead to mistrust, defiance, even rebellion" ("Perfect Love Casteth Out Fear," *Ensign*, May 2017; emphasis in original).

As we interrogate ourselves as to our motivations, we will identify and eliminate fear and allow it to be replaced by the love our Savior has for us, and our love for Him.

DESIRES TO CONTROL THE ACTIONS OF OTHERS

A less obvious way that we can avoid treating the Lord as someone whose actions can be manipulated by our own is to recognize that in responding to our prayerful desires, He will not abridge the agency of another person.

To choose an obviously silly example, when we pray that the latest pop star will come seek our hand in marriage, the Lord is not bound to force the celebrity to do so. But what about the cases in which our requests reflect righteous desires? For instance, a missionary who has come to love the person she is teaching may earnestly pray that the individual will seek and receive a confirming witness of the truth of the Book of Mormon and will decide to be baptized. The missionary's request is selfless; her heart desires that the very best blessings be available for her new friend. Nonetheless, the Lord will not violate the freedom of that individual to choose his own path. Recognition of this reality may change the missionary's prayer. She might plead instead to be guided to know the things to do and say that will create an environment more conducive to spiritual confirmations of that investigator's own prayers.

Earlier in my life, and over the period of several years, I prayed that the one I loved most would come to feel the same things I felt about the gospel of Jesus Christ. I prayed for that person to have a desire to act in order to learn the things that I was remembering and learning as I began again to participate in Church worship. I am confident my desired outcome would have been a great blessing in my companion's life, and yet the Lord could not have granted that plea without negating that wonderful person's own ideas and wishes. Eventually, I felt guided to pray simply that my loved one would find a path of happiness.

This is the point that President Henry B. Eyring made when he recounted a conversation he had with another (unnamed) Apostle:

> My promise to you is one that a member of the Quorum of the Twelve Apostles once made to me. I had said to him that because of choices some in our extended family had made, I doubted that we could be together in the world to come. He said, as well as I can remember, "You are worrying about the wrong problem. You just live worthy of the celestial kingdom, and the family arrangements will be more wonderful than you can imagine." ("A Home Where the Spirit of the Lord Dwells," *Ensign*, May 2019)

Even in our most loving and selfless desires for the benefit of others, our focus can productively be on seeking the Lord's help for us in our efforts, rather than seeking to specify His actions—and outcomes—in the life of another.

IN HIS TIME, IN HIS WAY

Another way I believe we can ensure we are not trying to manipulate God is to recognize that His omniscience includes knowing the best timing for His responses and blessings, whether in this life or in our next stage of existence. We know that "when we obtain any blessing from God, it is by obedience to that law upon which it is predicated" (Doctrine and Covenants 130:21). While we may rely on His promises, we cannot determine how or when He will fulfill them.

As Elder Dale G. Renlund has observed:

Remember that the "irrevocably decreed" law is time insensitive, meaning blessings come on God's timetable. Even ancient prophets in search of their heavenly home "died in faith, not having received the promises, but having seen them afar off, and were persuaded . . . and embraced them" [Hebrews 11:13]. If a desired blessing from God has not been received—yet—you do not need to go crazy, wondering what more you need to do. Instead, heed Joseph Smith's counsel to "cheerfully do all things that lie in [your] power; and then . . . stand still, with the utmost assurance, to see the . . . arm [of God] . . . revealed" [Doctrine and Covenants 123:17]. Some blessings are reserved for later, even for the most valiant of God's children. ("Abound with Blessings," *Ensign*, May 2019; see also Jeffrey R. Holland,

"An High Priest of Good Things to Come," *Ensign*, November 1999)

We pray with every fiber of faith we possess that a miracle of healing will be granted to a child battling cancer. And yet, in the end, we must accept that God's knowledge of what is best for that child is superior to our own. I believe there are circumstances when He will provide the blessing to *us* to be able to have continued relationship with another, to prolong or restore the life of that person whose life is even more dear to us than our own. In these moments when the only source of hope is the Lord, in addition to pleading with Him to intervene, we might equally plead that He will prepare our hearts to accept His will, and that His Spirit will attend us in our time of greatest need.

ALIGNING OUR WILL

Finally, the most critical step we can take in our desire to follow, not dictate to, the Lord is to align our wills with His. We do this not simply by adding "Thy will be done" to any request, but by actively working to know His will. Nephi, the son of Helaman, provides an example of the power and blessing that come with having our wills wholly subsumed by His: "And now, because thou hast done this with such unwearyingness, behold, I will bless thee forever; and I will make thee mighty in word and in deed, in faith and in works; yea, even that all things shall be done unto thee according to thy word, for thou shalt not ask that which is contrary to my will" (Helaman 10:5).

President Spencer W. Kimball was always a particular favorite of my mother's, not least because they had a shared experience of losing some of their vocal capacity due to surgical intervention to eradicate throat cancer. Mother's own voice had taken years to fully return, but she had forever lost the ability to sing or to shout. His biography relates his experiential learning that took place soon after his surgery as he traveled with his senior colleague in the Twelve, Elder Harold B. Lee. Elder Lee called on Elder Kimball to speak, which he did very briefly, after repeated attempts, with great difficulty and, I assume, some amount of painful discomfort.

The next day there was another meeting in Houston. Elder Lee, in charge, announced Elder Kimball as the next speaker. He stood and "made the most terrible sound you can imagine" until finally he found his voice and gave his sermon. Then he sat down, buried his head in his hands and mourned. "I was crying gallons of tears inside. I don't think they showed. But I really thought I was through, that I'd never preach again, that I wouldn't even try."

Three days later, driving by car to Texarkana, he passed Elder Lee a note: "I hope you won't embarrass me again." Elder Lee jovially responded, "Oh, I'm sure we'll call on you again. I think it's important for the people to hear your witness." Elder Kimball answered nothing. He knew he would do anything Elder Lee, his senior, asked. But inside he rebelled at the thought.

The conference at Texarkana was held in a long, narrow Methodist chapel. True to his word, Elder Lee called on his companion apostle to speak. It seemed impossible. The public address system was out. The chapel was huge. Outside the window was the highway, with trucks climbing a hill, grinding and shifting gears. Elder Kimball stood and began, "Brothers and

Sisters . . . " He prayed silently, he strained, the words came. For ten minutes he bore his testimony. Every person in the chapel heard him. He sat down and Elder Lee put his arm around him and said, "That's right, Spencer." (Edward L. Kimball and Andrew E. Kimball, *Spencer W. Kimball* [1977], 311–12)

King Benjamin provided some critical insight into the attributes that must accompany our efforts to align our will with the Lord's:

> For the natural man is an enemy to God, and has been from the fall of Adam, and will be, forever and ever, unless he yields to the enticings of the Holy Spirit, and putteth off the natural man and becometh a saint through the atonement of Christ the Lord, and becometh as a child, submissive, meek, humble, patient, full of love, willing to submit to all things which the Lord seeth fit to inflict upon him, even as a child doth submit to his father. (Mosiah 3:19)

Submissiveness is most certainly not a hallmark of the natural woman or man. We cannot simultaneously give the Lord our instructions for His actions while being willing to submit to Him in all things. We may discover as we strive to know Him, in order to become like Him, that our "wish lists" shrink and change, reflecting our desire for attributes rather than assets, characteristics in place of control, servitude instead of status. For changed hearts rather than changed circumstances.

CHAPTER SIX

SEEING HIS LOVE
IN TIMES OF TRIAL

Many of you are now passing through
physical, mental, and emotional trials
that could cause you to cry out
as did one great and faithful servant of God I knew well.
His nurse heard him exclaim from his bed of pain,
"When I have tried all my life to be good,
why has this happened to me?"

—President Henry B. Eyring, "Mountains to Climb," *Ensign*, May 2012

recall sitting in the Conference Center on Sunday morning, April 5, 2009. The concluding speaker of the session was President Thomas S. Monson. As he did so often and so well, President Monson illustrated his message with a life experience. He told of a young widow at the conclusion of the Second World War who was forced to flee on foot with four young children from East Prussia to Karlsruhe, a distance of about 1,000 miles. As President Monson shared the account of this sister's harrowing journey, his voice never faltered. Later, though, watching this conference address on a large-screen television, I could see tears roll down his cheeks as he related the account of this woman's terrible ordeal. In the freezing cold, death claimed her three-year-old daughter. But, "though overwhelmed with grief, she knew that she must take the other children and travel on. First, however, she used the only implement she had—a tablespoon—to dig a grave in the frozen ground for her tiny, precious child."

President Monson related that as the journey progressed, the woman's seven-year-old son died "from starvation or from freezing or both," soon to be followed by the five-year-old son, "and again she used her tablespoon as a shovel." Finally, her baby daughter also succumbed, and the only way left to her to provide a grave in the frozen soil was to dig with her fingers.

In this moment of overwhelming sorrow and complete bewilderment, she felt her heart would literally break. In despair she contemplated how she might end her own life, as so many of her fellow countrymen were doing. . . .

And then, as these thoughts assailed her, something within her said, "Get down on your knees and pray." She ignored the prompting until she could resist it no longer. She knelt and prayed more fervently than she had in her entire life:

"Dear Heavenly Father, I do not know how I can go on. I have nothing left—except my faith in Thee. I feel, Father, amidst the desolation of my soul, an overwhelming gratitude for the atoning sacrifice of Thy Son, Jesus Christ. I cannot express adequately my love for Him. I know that because He suffered and died, I shall live again with my family; that because He broke the chains of death, I shall see my children again and will have the joy of raising them. Though I do not at this moment wish to live, I will do so, that we may be reunited as a family and return—together—to Thee." ("Be of Good Cheer," *Ensign*, May 2009)

Is there any possible meaning we could understand in this tragedy—other than that a loving Father allowed the agency of others to proceed even with devasting impact to this daughter, knowing that in His time all would be made right? In the awful crucible of this journey, her knowledge of the plan of happiness would become perfected. That plan could only be brought to pass because another of His children, blameless and spotless, would make it possible.

How do we respond when we feel circumstances of our lives are unfair, impossible to bear, unjust?

First, we may recall that our trials can be a sign of our Heavenly Father's love and confidence in us: "My son, despise not the chastening of the Lord; neither be weary of his correction: For whom the Lord loveth he correcteth; even as a father the son in whom he delighteth" (Proverbs 3:11–12).

In the letter to the Hebrews traditionally ascribed to Paul, the author repeats that wisdom, and I particularly like the way Thomas A. Wayment has rendered it: "My child, do not disregard the Lord's discipline or be weary when reproved by him. For the Lord disciplines the one he loves and chastises every child whom he receives" (Hebrews 12:5–6, in Thomas A. Wayment, *The New Testament: A Translation for Latter-Day Saints* [2019]).

Surely this reality is another reason why we are commanded not to judge one another: what can look to us, as it did to Job's neighbors, like the reproof of God for disobedience may actually be a manifestation of His trust.

Second, we can acknowledge the truth that not all earthly challenges originate with God; many are the result of our own poor choices, and many are imposed by the choices of others. However, in humility and honesty, we can plead for all lessons the Lord would desire to teach us as we go through adversity. Our Heavenly Father may not change our circumstances, but, by changing our hearts, He can make it possible for us to endure, in order that we may learn.

> And it came to pass that the voice of the Lord came to them in their afflictions, saying: Lift up your heads and be of good comfort, for I know of the covenant which ye have made unto me; and I will covenant with my people and deliver them out of bondage.
>
> And I will also ease the burdens which are put upon your shoulders, that even you cannot feel them upon your backs, even while you are in bondage; and this will I do that ye may stand as witnesses for me hereafter, and that ye may know of a surety that I, the Lord God, do visit my people in their afflictions. (Mosiah 24:13–14)

Speaking of the Lord's goodness in helping us to change and to endure, Elder Kyle S. McKay noted, "Above all, God's love is immediate. With Paul, I testify that nothing can 'separate us from the love of God, which is in Christ Jesus' [Romans 8:39]. Even our sins, though they may separate us from His Spirit for a time, cannot separate us from the constancy and immediacy of His divine paternal love" ("The Immediate Goodness of God," *Ensign*, May 2019).

Sometimes trials may come not simply in the ordinary course of life, but because we have asked for them. I share this story with the permission of each of my brothers, as it is a sacred element of our birthright of faith from goodly parents. Our mother has written:

> When Wade was just tiny, I had a desire to draw closer to my Heavenly Father and husband. This desire increased to giant proportions while I was carrying Thomas and when he was newborn.

I wanted to be forgiven of all my past mistakes and shortcomings and to know that I was acceptable to the Lord. I also wanted to come closer to my husband. We had a good marriage by the world's standards, but there was a holding back a bit of ourselves on both sides and I desired for us to truly become "one."

For much of a year I prayed constantly—when not on my knees, in my heart—with a constant prayer for forgiveness and courage to truly be one with the Lord and with [my husband] Paul.

Six months after I was born, my mother was diagnosed with a malignant cancer that had spread into all the tissue surrounding her thyroid glands, and immediate preparations were begun for surgery the next morning. She recorded, "They took out all the tissue, muscles and jugular vein, from the right side of my neck, as well as some of the voice box and parts of a couple cervical vertebrae on the shoulder, front and back, down almost to the chest."

Our father stayed in the hospital, sleeping on a cot next to her bed, for ten days. Our mother relates that a few days post-surgery she developed pneumonia, and her already precarious condition rapidly deteriorated.

[My sister] Adena Nell kept reading out loud the blessing that my father had given me before I entered the hospital. It told me that I would live through the operation. The splotches of her tears are still on it. She left for home around 9 p.m. Towards morning, Dr. [Wallace] Sorenson told Paul he should call for my parents to come because the end was near. He asked if Paul would like him to stay in the room or wait outside the door. Paul asked him to leave us alone.

[Paul] knelt and prayed to have the courage to let me go, if that was the Lord's will. I whispered my love and said I couldn't hold on anymore. He began to sob, "Oh dear God, how can I tell our boys?" I asked him to hold me tight as I couldn't hold myself together alone. He sat on the bed and held me in his arms for a long time. As the dawn started to break, we both knew the Lord had blessed us and my life would be spared. We knew it would be hard, but we never doubted I would make it.

Our mother concluded her remembrance with these words:

The most important [thing] that I can record was the blessing of closeness and openness that Paul and I reached with each other. The ability to give completely to each other our love, thoughts and desires. And, oh the blessed feeling to know that my life was acceptable before the Lord, that my sins and transgressions were wiped away in repentance. I was so close to the Lord all the time I was in the hospital and for the weeks following when I was receiving my twenty-six x-ray treatments. I wish I could describe in words the experiences of that time. The Lord was so close to me that I know had it been necessary I could have seen Him. I know this is true with every fiber of my being and I testify of its truth. Paul also had these same blessings: may we both live worthy to be together in the Lord's presence with that same feeling of worthiness is our constant prayer and aim. (Jeanne S. Christofferson, unpublished manuscript, 1994)

I hope you will understand the feelings in the hearts of their sons when I share our confident assurance that our dear parents endured to the end of their lives with all the worthiness for which our mother had prayed. One of the ways that I have learned of the pure love of

Christ is through the daily example of my parents, reflected not only in how they treated their sons and families, but also in their interactions with everyone who crossed their paths in life. In many ways, they were the most ordinary of people, and yet because of their sure faith in Christ and His Father, because they built the whole of their lives on that certainty, they lived extraordinary lives.

Perhaps the greatest blessing the Lord has in store during times of adversity is to change our hearts, rather than changing our afflictions. The people of King Limhi were not immediately delivered from their difficulties, but the Lord did begin to soften the hearts of the Lamanites so that they would ease the burdens they imposed. Many trials last years and even decades, and as we come to rely increasingly on the Lord, like Limhi's people, we come to trust that He will provide daily strength and support even when we cannot see any near-term resolution to our difficulties. Our desires imperceptibly change. That is the promise of Ezekiel, repeated in Hebrews:

> And I will give them one heart, and I will put a new spirit within you; and I will take the stony heart out of their flesh, and will give them an heart of flesh: That they may walk in my statutes, and keep mine ordinances, and do them: and they shall be my people, and I will be their God. (Ezekiel 11:19–20)

> For this is the covenant that I will make with the house of Israel after those days, saith the Lord; I will put my laws into their mind, and write them in their hearts: and I will be to them a God, and they shall be to me a people: And they shall not teach every man his neighbour, and every man his brother, saying, Know the Lord: for all shall know me, from the least to the greatest. For I will be merciful to their unrighteousness,

and their sins and their iniquities will I remember no more.
(Hebrews 8:10–12)

A heart that desires the things of God, that has learned to love
what and how He loves, is both a blessing in its own right and an indi-
cation of the covenant that our Father has made with us. Perhaps the
Lord is able to be merciful to us as imperfect individuals partly because
He knows our desires to do better, our prayerful intention to follow
Him, and our gratitude for the love He constantly shows for us.

But what of the circumstances when an individual has knowingly
inflicted pain and suffering on us? What of physical or mental abuse,
theft or embezzlement, or even more serious and irreversible crimes?
Where do we find the Lord in those circumstances? We are all aware
of incredible stories of grace in which, for example, the parents of a
child who has been killed in an automobile accident due to volun-
tary impairment by the other driver have demonstrated extraordinary
willingness to forgive and even to help the person who was the instrument of their child's death. Those instances ennoble us all and make
us grateful for the example of such individuals. The healing they have
received from the Lord through His Holy Spirit brings peace to an
entire community.

President James E. Faust related a powerful story about the Amish
people in Nickel Mines, Pennsylvania:

> A 32-year-old milk truck driver lived with his family in their
> Nickel Mines community. He was not Amish, but his pickup
> route took him to many Amish dairy farms, where he became
> known as the quiet milkman. Last October he suddenly lost all
> reason and control. In his tormented mind he blamed God for

the death of his first child and some unsubstantiated memories. He stormed into the Amish school without any provocation, released the boys and adults, and tied up the 10 girls. He shot the girls, killing five and wounding five. Then he took his own life.

This shocking violence caused great anguish among the Amish but no anger. There was hurt but no hate. Their forgiveness was immediate. Collectively they began to reach out to the milkman's suffering family. As the milkman's family gathered in his home the day after the shootings, an Amish neighbor came over, wrapped his arms around the father of the dead gunman, and said, "We will forgive you." Amish leaders visited the milkman's wife and children to extend their sympathy, their forgiveness, their help, and their love. About half of the mourners at the milkman's funeral were Amish. In turn, the Amish invited the milkman's family to attend the funeral services of the girls who had been killed. A remarkable peace settled on the Amish as their faith sustained them during this crisis. ("The Healing Power of Forgiveness," *Ensign*, May 2007)

For others, though, peace and healing take much longer, despite equally fervent prayers and effort. Getting out of bed and putting one foot in front of the other can be acts of supreme courage and faith.

We can feel a desire for revenge, hate can grow in our hearts and cause our own growth to be stalled, all because someone else acted ignominiously. Forgiveness in some cases may require years of assistance from talented therapists, counsel with patient and wise Church leaders, and the constant and consoling presence of friends and family members. Reassurance that the spiritual miracle of healing can eventually come may be most convincingly received from those who have shared similar experiences.

For most of us, thankfully, our challenges are less dire. We might have a work colleague who acts in ways that challenge our ability to perform, or a friend or acquaintance who spreads false stories about us, or a family member who is repeatedly unkind and seemingly unrepentant. Whatever the cause of distress, we can be left with a feeling that someone has chosen to act as an enemy, and fairness dictates that there should be punishment. Perhaps we conjure elaborate ways that we can be avenged. Or we pepper Heavenly Father with our demands that He should exact justice on the one who has thus wounded us. Perhaps, on some level, we recognize the truth in the old adage, "Before you embark on a journey of revenge, dig two graves." We might acknowledge that hatred and anger can wreak more havoc on us than on the object of our fury. But despite our knowledge that our ability to hear the Spirit, to feel connected to Heavenly Parents and our Savior, is impeded when hate enters our hearts, still, at times, it can feel beyond our capacity to let go of the hurt.

Likely you are familiar with the true story of the Casper ten Boom family of the Netherlands. During World War II, they sheltered many Jews from the Nazis, enabling their escape, but eventually the ten Booms were caught and arrested. The father died soon after, but sisters Corrie and Betsie were imprisoned in the Ravensbrück concentration camp. In her autobiography, *The Hiding Place,* Corrie relates that she and her sister held Christian worship services, using a Bible they had smuggled in.

One day in the camp, Corrie and Betsie saw a guard "mercilessly beating a female prisoner. 'What can we do for these people?' Corrie whispered. 'Show them that love is greater,' Betsie replied. In that moment, Corrie realized her sister's focus was on the prison guard, not the victim she was watching. Betsie saw the world through a different lens. She considered the actions of greatest moral gravity to be the ones we originate, not the ones we suffer" (Terryl Givens and Fiona Givens, *The God Who Weeps: How Mormonism Makes Sense of Life* [2012], 80).

I doubt I would have been wise enough, sufficiently consecrated in my own discipleship, to have intuited that lesson. My reaction would more likely have been fear and dread, if not plain numbness. Betsie had fully absorbed the teaching of Paul: "For God hath not given us the spirit of fear; but of power, and of love, and of a sound mind" (2 Timothy 1:7).

How might we train ourselves to be filled with His love, to have a better heart as well as an agile mind?

May I suggest periodically making time to read, consider, and absorb the lessons found in the twenty-fifth chapter of Matthew? Jesus shares three parables in that chapter, drawing with ever-greater precision the lesson He is teaching, in much the same way that geometry uses triangulation to precisely determine the location of a point.

He begins with the parable of the Wise and Foolish Maidens (or Virgins, in the King James translation). This parable is a common reference point in our gospel teaching. We are given to understand that the oil in the maidens' lamps represents faith or the testimony of truth. Long before the moment of need arrives, the work and effort must be accomplished to gain such a personal witness, to become fluent in the workings of the Spirit, able both to receive and to understand revelation. Those spiritual gifts cannot be simply dropped off at someone else's door or borrowed; they can be gained only through personal performance. I find the clearest way for me to understand this point is to think of the changed heart that Jesus has promised as we diligently try to become as He is. That heart also represents the love I have gained for Christ as I have come to understand who He is and what He has done for me. It is a striking, if grisly, metaphor to imagine how, despite overwhelming desire, I might successfully divide and share physical portions of my heart with another.

The second parable concerns the Talents. As others have pointed out, because the name for this particular unit of money is translated into English as a "talent," we often substitute in our minds its homonym, meaning ability or gift. As you read the parable this time, think of talents as a currency that would represent quite a large sum of money to us today. When the master gives a talent (let alone two or five talents) to his servants, he is entrusting them with something we should understand to have enormous value, perhaps millions of dollars. We know the story: when the master returns from his journey, the servants who have enhanced the value of their lord's money are praised and told they have brought him joy, in which they will now share. Finally, we come to the servant to whom had been consigned one measure. His report to the master—"I knew thee that thou art an hard man, reaping where thou hast not sown, and gathering where thou hast not strawed" (Matthew 25:24), which led him to do nothing to nurture and care for the precious talent—indicates that he does not know his lord at all.

As you consider layers of meaning within this story, substitute in your mind for the unit of currency something valuable to you. For example, you and your spouse might embark on a business trip and leave your children in the care of a family member or close friend. You have entrusted that which is most dear to you, and you would plead with the one acting in your behalf to nourish and care with great tenderness for your treasures. Upon your return, you would indeed be joyful to find your children thriving in the watch care of your "servant," and equally, you would be heartbroken to find a child who had been left to fend for himself, unwatched, unguarded, unloved. Consider Heavenly Father as the Master and the reality of Christ as His not only uncared-for, but abused and harmed Child. Or imagine our Redeemer as the Master and yourself as the child.

The third and final parable is that of the Sheep and Goats, which offers a poignant reminder that if we fail to care for the needy among us, we cannot inherit our Father's kingdom.

As you consider how each parable builds on what has gone before to sharpen our understanding of what Jesus is seeking to teach, I believe you will feel more deeply than ever that His lesson is love. More precisely, He is teaching of His love for us, which He desires we also should feel for our brothers and sisters. His love is evidenced by joy upon knowing that those who follow Him have compassionately cared for their fellows, and sorrow that one has not understood His mission. His love is what five wise maidens have gained and carried in their lamps. His love is the treasure, measured in units of one, two, and five. His love for each of us as wounded travelers on our journey through mortality restores life, through universal resurrection as well as spiritual rebirth, if we are willing to become as He is.

Lest we have somehow misunderstood, in some of the most beautiful language in all of scripture, the chapter concludes with perfect clarity: that which we do to or for one another, we truly do for Him.

Then shall the King say unto them on his right hand, Come, ye blessed of my Father, inherit the kingdom prepared for you from the foundation of the world: For I was an hungred, and ye gave me meat: I was thirsty, and ye gave me drink: I was a stranger, and ye took me in: Naked, and ye clothed me: I was sick, and ye visited me: I was in prison, and ye came unto me.

Then shall the righteous answer him, saying, Lord, when saw we thee an hungred, and fed thee? or thirsty, and gave thee drink? When saw we thee a stranger, and took thee in? or naked, and clothed thee? Or when saw we thee sick, or in prison, and came unto thee?

And the King shall answer and say unto them, Verily I say unto you, Inasmuch as ye have done it unto one of the least of these my brethren, ye have done it unto me. (Matthew 25:34–40)

When we are fully imbued with His lesson, the idea that another might be "less" becomes unimaginable. Think of the description of the perfected inhabitants of the city of Enoch: "And the Lord called his people Zion, because they were of one heart and one mind, and dwelt in righteousness; and there was no poor among them" (Moses 7:18). The entire seventh chapter of the book of Moses is worth careful contemplation. When Enoch marvels that one so holy and complete as the Lord can weep, he is told:

Behold these thy brethren; they are the workmanship of mine own hands, and I gave unto them their knowledge, in the day I created them; and in the Garden of Eden, gave I unto man his agency; And unto thy brethren have I said, and also given commandment, that they should love one another, and that they should choose me, their Father; but behold, they are without affection, and they hate their own blood. (Moses 7:32–33)

As He taught Enoch, so He tutored Joseph: "And in nothing doth man offend God, or against none is his wrath kindled, save those who confess not his hand in all things, and obey not his commandments" (Doctrine and Covenants 59:21).

And what are His commandments? The two He identified as greatest require that we love His Father and that we love our neighbors as ourselves. From Matthew 25 and Moses 7, we comprehend that if we would avoid causing our Lord sorrow, if we desire not to offend Him, then we must act in His love toward every person we encounter. He will respond to our greatest desire: He will grant the gift of charity, His pure love, as we consistently and earnestly seek it.

And that, finally, is the service of suffering, and why His complete compassion will not allow Him to spare us from even devastating impact. In that crucible, a shadow of Gethsemane, we come to experience and then gain transformative love. Like a night sky deep in a desert, no terrestrial gleam obscures the limitless abundance of gentle light, bringing peace, possibilities beyond imagination, a unity of one soul with all souls. This is divine love—not the precursor found in romance, devotion, or mere obedience, but rather, that which transforms faith into knowledge, which renews lives, families, and communities, and grants the formation of a new and better heart, one that beats in rhythm with His.

CHAPTER SEVEN

FINDING THE SPIRIT OF LOVE IN THE LAW

But in all these things, we are more than conquerors through him who loved us.
For I am convinced that neither death nor life nor angels nor heavenly rulers
nor things that are present nor things to come nor powers
nor height nor depth nor anything else in creation
will be able to separate us from the love of God in Christ Jesus our Lord.

—Romans 8:37–38, in Thomas A. Wayment,
The New Testament: A Translation for Latter-day Saints (2018)

O ne memorable evening, I invited my friend Megan Beus to speak to the single adult ward study group. We were studying the final week of Jesus's life in Jerusalem, and in particular His celebration of Passover with His Apostles, which we more frequently refer to as the Last Supper. Megan shared some of the key prayers and rituals associated with the Seder, and her insights deepened our understanding and appreciation for that signal event in Christ's life. As she concluded, she mentioned the experience of Rabbi Aharon Davids in the Bergen-Belsen concentration camp in Germany in 1944. His faith in God, even in the direst of circumstances, was profoundly moving, and over subsequent days I found myself eagerly searching for anything I could find about his life.

I share the historical account of Rabbi Davids's experience with some hesitation, as it treads on the sacred ground of the Holocaust. I am in reverent awe of the goodness of these people in circumstances that are unimaginable yet real. This true story has enhanced my perception of those whose wholehearted reverence for God's law is inextricably entwined with a sense of His love at its core.

Rabbi Davids was serving as the Chief Rabbi of Rotterdam, Netherlands, when the Nazis deported the entire Jewish community, eventually sending them to the Bergen-Belsen concentration camp in northern Germany. Conditions were awful beyond imagination: current estimates put the number of deaths at Belsen at more than 50,000 Jews, Czechs, Poles, anti-Nazi Christians, homosexuals, and Roma and Sinti (Gypsies), in addition to approximately 20,000 Russian prisoners of war.

An important element in the Passover celebration is *matzah,* unleavened bread. One reason for its use at that time is as a reminder of the "bread of affliction" the Jewish people ate while slaves in Egypt, as well as the bread that did not have time to rise as Moses, acting as commanded by the Lord, led his people out of captivity and into freedom. As Passover approached in 1944, it was obvious that the Jewish prisoners would have no access to *matzah*; indeed they scarcely had enough leavened bread (*chametz*) to eat among the starvation-level rations provided by their captors.

It was this dilemma—how to observe the law of Moses to foreswear *chametz* during this sacred time without causing additional starvation among his fellow prisoners—with which Rabbi Davids wrestled in faith.

A former president of the state of Israel, Reuvin Rivlin, spoke at the Yad Vashem Holocaust Memorial in Jerusalem in April 2016, on the eve of Holocaust Martyrs' and Heroes' Remembrance Day of that year. Among his remarks, Rivlin said:

> On the night of the Passover Seder, 1944, in barrack 18 of the Bergen Belsen Concentration Camp, a group of Jewish prisoners gathered, determined not to eat Chametz. . . . Rabbi Aharon Bernard (Yisachar) Davids . . . explained to them that it was their obligation to do what was necessary to stay alive. In order to convince them, he picked up a piece of bread, and before eating it on that Seder night, he read a special prayer which he had penned together with Rabbi Simon Dasbergm, and other Rabbis from Holland, which read:
>
> "Our Father in Heaven! It is known to You that we desire to fulfill Your will and observe the Passover holiday by eating Matzah and safeguarding against Chametz. But our hearts are pained at the captivity which prevents us, and we find ourselves in danger of our lives. We are hereby ready to fulfill Your commandments, 'And you shall live by them (the commandments)' and not die by them, and to observe the caution of 'guard yourself and watch your soul/life very much.' Therefore our prayer to You is that You keep us alive, and sustain us, and redeem us speedily." ("Address by President of the State of Israel, H.E. Mr. Reuven Rivlin: State Opening Ceremony of Holocaust Martyrs' and Heroes' Remembrance Day 2016"; https://www.yadvashem .org/remembrance/archive/address-by-president/2016.html)

Rabbi Davids and his son died before the concentration camp was liberated. His wife, Erika, and their daughters survived and later emigrated to Israel. She was able to take with her a copy of her husband's prayer, and it can now be seen in the Ghetto Fighters Museum in Tel-Aviv.

Can you feel in Rabbi Davids's prayer that he was reaching toward the love he found in God's commandment? Can you recognize this good man's certainty that it would be the opposite of that love to prohibit what little sustenance was provided in order to avoid what the law proscribed?

That prayer, and the understanding that God would have us live by His commandments and not die by them, has become a sacred touchstone in many contemporary Seder celebrations. It provides an opportunity for each one of us to contemplate how we find the Lord's love in His commandments, in both the spirit and the letter of His laws.

Sometimes I reach rather easily for Paul's words from Second Corinthians, "For the letter killeth, but the spirit giveth life" (2 Corinthians 3:6). The temptation exists to disregard what I have promised to do, excusing my actions with a blithe notion that the spirit always trumps the letter. But if I seek to identify the Lord's love in observance of a commandment, I am likely to come closer to understanding its spiritual purpose. As the life of Rabbi Davids, blessed be his memory, witnesses to us, we desire to obey both the letter and spirit of our covenants, and perhaps only *in extremis*, when our desires are righteous, is there a dichotomy between the two.

Perhaps another way to conceive our desire to discern the Lord's loving purposes in His laws, as well as their spiritual underpinnings, is to imagine yourself walking through the gardens of a large public park. As you walk, you're aware of the varying colors, textures, maturity, and types of flowers, plants, and trees. For the briefest of moments, you catch the scent of jasmine, its perfume heady in the air and then suddenly gone as you continue to stroll. That short, sweet moment of awareness, familiar, alluring, can be a type of the Lord's gentle, tender call to know Him and discover His loving intent within His laws.

Desiring, striving, to absorb both the letter *and* the spirit of love in the law can remind us of what is truly central to our doctrine, commandments, and covenants. In the words of Joseph Smith:

> The fundamental principles of our religion are the testimony of the Apostles and Prophets, concerning Jesus Christ, that He died, was buried, and rose again the third day, and ascended into heaven; and all other things which pertain to our religion are only appendages to it. But in connection with these, we believe in the gift of the Holy Ghost, the power of faith, the enjoyment of the spiritual gifts according to the will of God, the restoration of the house of Israel, and the final triumph of truth. (*History of the Church*, 7 volumes [1932–1951], 3:30)

As I've contemplated this, it seems to me that we need to consider more dimensions of questions that face us, rather than simply thinking of "letter versus spirit." I believe our decisions will be enriched if we also think about being "almost" versus "altogether" converted, to use the words of Paul from his testimony before King Agrippa. After teaching of Jesus as the Christ, of His Resurrection, and of His light upon Jews and Gentiles, Paul challenges:

> King Agrippa, believest thou the prophets? I know that thou believest. Then Agrippa said unto Paul [those heartbreaking words], Almost thou persuadest me to be a Christian. And Paul said, I would to God, that not only thou, but also all that

hear me this day, were both almost, and altogether such as I am, except these bonds. (Acts 26:27–29)

We can be almost converted, almost observant of covenants and commandments, or we can be altogether engaged, holding nothing back from God. That complete conversion, I believe, comes as a result of fully understanding and absorbing the Lord's love, and therefore having our love for Him be the driving impetus of our obedience.

In line with Paul's use of *almost* and *altogether* converted, I've tried to engage this concept with the notion of the letter and spirit of the law in a graph. Almost and Altogether are on the Y axis, and the Letter and Spirit of the law on the X axis.

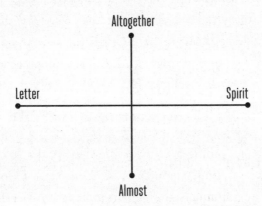

Before we discuss the various quadrants in the graph, please recognize that it is more focused on actions than on desires. And we understand that the perfect Judge of us all values our desires as well as our actions and knows the context of our circumstances and abilities. In particular, there can be perfectly understandable reasons why desire must suffice for action. For example, people who suffer from depression may be hyperaware of what they desire to be doing even as the malady robs them of the strength to actually accomplish it. If there is any worth in this exercise, it really exists only as an invitation to think about where I want to be and how I can focus my efforts more consistently in that direction.

We begin with the bottom left quadrant, the one that is low in following the letter of the law and almost converted in obedience. In this quadrant, we might be knowledgeable about specific covenants and commandments and perhaps speak of them with great precision—especially when looking at the actions of others—without any congruent behavior on our own part. I think it is a lack of experience with Christ's love that robs us of a driving impetus to act rather than to simply prescribe for others our view of how they should act. This quadrant represents a rather strange combination of awareness and laziness. Perhaps we experience times in our lives when our consciences remind us of what we should be doing, but we can't quite summon the willpower to do it.

Next door, the quadrant on the lower right, represents high attachment to the spirit of laws and covenants with an almost observant approach to living according to those impressions of the Spirit. Here we might feel that we understand the loving purpose of God's laws and covenants, yet that understanding fails to drive a higher degree of implementation; we do not turn our cognition into action. I think in this quadrant we might be hesitant—because of our understanding of the spiritual dimension of God's laws—to call out and criticize others for their behavior. This is progress from the lower left quadrant, at least, but it still indicates a failure to put our knowledge into practice.

The upper quadrant on the left-hand side represents altogether committed observance, but with a focus on the letter of the law.

Perhaps this indicates a desire for a checklist of actions by which we can certify our personal worthiness every day. As with its partner in the quadrant below, the missing link seems to be an understanding that commandments arise from God's love and require our love for Him in order to drive action worthy of His purposes. There is likely not a high level of outward focus in this quadrant, unless it is on comparing one's own careful observance with that of neighbors. Here we expend a great deal of energy and worry on perfection in small things. I sometimes think of this as adhering to The Church of the Word of Wisdom or The Church of No Male Facial Hair, as opposed to The Church of Jesus Christ. Here may also be found actions motivated by fear rather than love, a focus on outward appearance rather than on a broken heart and contrite spirit.

Finally, the upper right-hand quadrant represents what we are striving for: a high level of guidance by the Spirit accompanied by an altogether converted approach to all that is revealed to us. Whereas the concept of "altogether obedience" represents real danger in the upper left-hand quadrant, here such obedience brings light and knowledge. It produces increased faith and greater conversion to the benefit of all, not solely the individual, because it is engendered by love for and from our Savior. When we act in this quadrant, we glorify God rather than ourselves. This is where priesthood power is actualized to bless the lives of our sisters and brothers. Our focus has become the alignment of our wills with that of Christ and of our Father. Our desires for prestige and acknowledgment have been replaced with meekness and a yearning to be chastened, corrected, and taught. Truly understanding the scope and purpose of covenants we have made has given us a freedom to focus on the incredible love of our Heavenly

Parents and our Redeemer, as evidenced by Their gifts of mortal life and the possibility of eternal life. In conjunction with this quadrant, I think of the description of the inhabitants of the city of Enoch: "And the Lord called his people Zion, because they were of one heart and one mind, and dwelt in righteousness; and there was no poor among them" (Moses 7:18).

I hope the thought exercise with this graph is useful to you.

A New Testament example of how observing and following the law is enlivened and given purpose by its loving spiritual purpose may be useful. The Pentecost observance prescribed by the law of Moses is a time to rejoice and to observe: *Shavuot,* a celebration of the first fruits of the harvest, and *Matin Torah,* commemorating the giving of the law through Moses to the children of Israel. Peter and his fellow Apostles, celebrating the first Pentecost following Christ's Resurrection, witnessed the intensity of, and gained the companionship of, the Holy Spirit in great power. Evidences of His presence among these Galilean speakers included the capacity to testify to others, from "every nation under heaven" (Acts 2:5), in their own languages, "that God hath made that same Jesus, whom ye have crucified, both Lord and Christ" (Acts 2:36). This miraculous commencement of the original Church of Jesus Christ, led by prophets and apostles, occurred in the context of appreciative celebration for the first fruit from God (a type and symbol of Jesus) and for His law (which Jesus as Jehovah had given). Our experience can be the same. We also can be filled with His Spirit as we give thanks for the gift of a Savior and Redeemer. His commandments and covenants, signs of His love for us, change our hearts as we turn toward Him.

To conclude this examination of the spirit and letter of the law,

I thought to share a more current example, one from my own life. It was a small thing in the scheme of life, but this lesson has expanded both my thinking and my determination to act in ways that reflect my love for my Savior.

When I returned to Church activity a dozen or so years ago, I had a couple of conversations with the bishop of the ward about home teaching. Because I was not a member at that time, I obviously could not be called to be a home teacher, but I wondered whether someone might be assigned responsibility to visit me. I came to understand that the home teaching program by definition was focused on Church members caring for other members. Over time I came to feel that when I identified opportunities to serve, I could imagine that I was creating my own home teaching route, and I delighted in that opportunity of ad hoc service (without reporting requirements).

After being baptized, I was given a home teaching companion and families to watch over. I came to love the people I got to know in this way, but I often felt that I was coming up short as a home teacher. The home teaching success stories shared in priesthood meeting seemed to be about a wonderful brother who fixed the roof of a family home when the father was traveling on business, or the brother who got up before daybreak to shovel a family's driveway so the wife could fulfill her calling as the early-morning seminary teacher, or the brother who attended every athletic event of each of the children in the families he visited. No one has ever accused me of being a handyman, and my own work-related travel was extensive at that time, so from one week to the next I couldn't predict when I would be available to do something at my own home, let alone the home of a family for whom I had been given stewardship. (And I had a sneaking suspicion that no kid would be delighted to see me sitting in the bleachers reading a book because I was so bored by the game!)

When President Russell M. Nelson announced a "newer, holier approach to caring for and ministering to others" ("Ministering," *Ensign*, May 2018), I thought I understood the differences this way of ministering represented from earlier, more programmatic approaches, and I was happy to try to fulfill my calling in this manner. With the benefit of hindsight, however, I realize that what had been revealed to prophets, apostles, and the General Presidencies of the Relief Society and Young Women provided, for me, a way to clear away the clutter of performing tasks and instead to focus more diligently on love. I came to understand that being called to minister in His name reflected His love for His children now in my stewardship, as well as His love for me, as He entrusted me with a charge to expand my capabilities to transmit that love in every interaction, an understanding I had somehow missed as a home teacher.

I have realized that when my companion and I join one of our ministering families to go get frozen custard, taking time to laugh and enjoy each other, we are living our love for each other. When my ministering brothers take me out to eat at a Mexican restaurant in my new neighborhood, in addition to helping me adjust to a new home, they are living their love for me. I have found that praying by name for each member of the families my companion and I minister to is something I look forward to. Feeling freed of the constraints of a program in my own mind—constraints that need never have been there—I have been able to concentrate on getting to know each person, finding common interests, and trying to discern unique needs. Those who truly fulfilled their callings as home or visiting teachers intrinsically understood the mandate to minister, but I had limited my own thinking to only the outward performance.

One example of my changed approach occurred as we were finishing the final chapters of the four Gospels in the New Testament as part of our *Come, Follow Me* study plan. One of our ministering families has younger children at home, baptized but not yet teenagers. That week, as I was reading the chapters, I felt a great desire to have a short visit with that family so I could share my witness that Jesus was indeed resurrected, that He is real, and He lives and leads His Church today. That Sunday was the last day of the month. In the home teaching program, I could have been embarrassed, as all of us might have thought that this visit was a means to check a box at the last possible moment. But as a ministering brother, I was eager to have a brief conversation with these people whom I love dearly, and who are so kind to me. As I shared my testimony, the father of the family also shared his, and the Spirit was present to convey our words to the hearts of each person. As I got back to my home afterward, I dropped to my knees to thank my Heavenly Father for inspired leaders, and for this window I had been given to see His love so vividly. The real ministering service that day had come from Him, as it always does, and my life was blessed by a small effort, guided by love, to represent Him.

Even with that gratitude, I know that I am capturing only a portion of what the Lord would have me do as one who ministers in His place. There is so much I leave undone each day. And yet, I remain humbly appreciative for His trust that tomorrow, or during the next interaction, or next year, I will be a clearer line of transmission for His love. I am grateful for the hope I feel that ministering is something I can do, even in my tiny sphere and my imperfect way, that contributes to building His kingdom and gathering His sheep.

General Relief Society President Jean B. Bingham astutely taught:

> After all is said and done, true ministering is accomplished one by one with love as the motivation. The value and merit and wonder of sincere ministering is that it truly changes lives! When our hearts are open and willing to love and include, encourage and comfort, the power of our ministering will be irresistible. With love as the motivation, miracles will happen, and we will find ways to bring our "missing" sisters and brothers into the all-inclusive embrace of the gospel of Jesus Christ. ("Ministering as the Savior Does," *Ensign*, May 2018)

President Bingham's words clearly capture the truth that a formal calling to minister is accomplished only when a heart has been made better by the love from Him whose service we are in, and is thus capable of acting in that love as He would in that instant.

We began the chapter memorializing the extraordinary life of one such minister, Rabbi Davids, a life marked by courage and illuminated by love of God, by devotion to His laws, and by tender stewardship of his congregants in a crucible of suffering. Our respect for such agony of body and spirit must constantly enliven within us a determination that hatred can never again be the driving force of a nation or world, that better hearts will prevail.

CHAPTER EIGHT

COMMANDMENTS ARE LOVE

For the Father himself loveth you,
because ye have loved me,
and have believed that I came out from God.

—John 16:27

Have you ever performed the thought exercise of asking yourself not only why is loving God the greatest commandment, and loving neighbor is of similar importance, but also why would Jesus say that "on these two commandments hang all the law and the prophets" (Matthew 22:40)?

The literal meaning of *the law and the prophets* that Jesus's contemporary audience would have understood refers to the two sections of the Jewish scriptures. The *law* (of Moses) consists of the books of Genesis, Exodus, Leviticus, Numbers, and Deuteronomy. The view of what is included in the section called *prophets* varies among denominations but perhaps could be thought of as the remaining Old Testament texts, excluding books considered "writings," such as Psalms, Proverbs, Lamentations, Ecclesiastes, and others. One way of rephrasing what Jesus said would be that all of the scriptures with which He and His audience were so familiar were meant to prepare the world for Him, the One who would accomplish the greatest offering of love ever seen.

The law of Moses contains 613 commandments, or rules or good acts. We are most familiar with what we have come to call the Ten Commandments.

> Thou shalt have no other gods before me.
>
> Thou shalt not make unto thee any graven image, or any likeness of any thing that is in heaven above, or that is in the earth beneath, or that is in the water under the earth. . . .
>
> Thou shalt not take the name of the Lord thy God in vain; for the Lord will not hold him guiltless that taketh his name in vain.
>
> Remember the sabbath day, to keep it holy. . . .
>
> Honour thy father and thy mother: that thy days may be long upon the land which the Lord thy God giveth thee.
>
> Thou shalt not kill.
>
> Thou shalt not commit adultery.
>
> Thou shalt not steal.
>
> Thou shalt not bear false witness against thy neighbour.
>
> Thou shalt not covet thy neighbour's house, thou shalt not covet thy neighbour's wife, nor his manservant, nor his maidservant, nor his ox, nor his ass, nor any thing that is thy neighbour's. (Exodus 20:3–4, 7–8, 12–17)

If we think of the two great commandments as incorporating all other laws, we can do a quick test with these ten. Knowing and worshiping solely the One True God, and doing so with all of our hearts, minds, and souls, would represent fidelity to the first four of the Ten Commandments. Truly loving our neighbors—or, in other words, loving, respecting, and honoring the birthright of all the children of our Heavenly Parents—would demonstrate our commitment to the remaining six commandments.

I believe you will find the same to be true of any other commandments you might consider, such as the law of the fast or the law of tithing. Our faithful devotion to these laws reflects our willingness to worship the God who has given them to us. For example, when you fully participate in a fast, when you have consciously begun it with prayer, when you are seeking for the Spirit to teach you during that period, when you ponder the blessings you seek for yourself or others, when you search scriptures for insight and revelation, when your attention is captured not by how many hours remain of the fast nor by what food will be included in the next meal but by how you may serve others, and when you conclude your fast with grateful and specific prayer, you know that the fast given by God is a gift and not a burden. Your gratitude for the experience increases your willingness and desire to worship the Giver of the Law.

In both of these cases, the fast and tithing, our love of God expressed through our obedience also blesses our neighbors. I have come to feel that if my focus is on the two great commandments, everything else will fall into place.

During my career, I had the wonderful opportunity to serve for several years on the advisory board for the political action committee of one of the largest corporations in America. As a member of that board, I participated in meetings with many well-known political leaders of the United States and a few leaders of other nations. I was particularly intrigued while meeting with these women and men "up close and personal" to note how many seemed to have great regard for the needs of people in general and very little interest in or patience for individuals. What a stark contrast to the Lord's way of treating people!

I resonate with the experience related in the Gospel of Luke of Jesus and the woman who "loved much":

And one of the Pharisees desired him that he would eat with him. And he went into the Pharisee's house, and sat down to meat.

And, behold, a woman in the city, which was a sinner, when she knew that Jesus sat at meat in the Pharisee's house, brought an alabaster box of ointment,

And stood at his feet behind him weeping, and began to wash his feet with tears, and did wipe them with the hairs of her head, and kissed his feet, and anointed them with the ointment.

Now when the Pharisee which had bidden him saw it, he spake within himself, saying, This man, if he were a prophet, would have known who and what manner of woman this is that toucheth him: for she is a sinner.

And Jesus answering said unto him, Simon, I have somewhat to say unto thee. And he saith, Master, say on.

There was a certain creditor which had two debtors: the one owed five hundred pence, and the other fifty. And when they had nothing to pay, he frankly forgave them both. Tell me therefore, which of them will love him most?

Simon answered and said, I suppose that he, to whom he forgave most. And he said unto him, Thou hast rightly judged. And he turned to the woman, and said unto Simon, Seest thou this woman? I entered into thine house, thou gavest me no water for my feet: but she hath washed my feet with tears, and wiped them with the hairs of her head. Thou gavest me no kiss: but this woman since the time I came in hath not ceased to kiss my feet.

My head with oil thou didst not anoint: but this woman hath anointed my feet with ointment.

Wherefore I say unto thee, Her sins, which are many, are forgiven; for she loved much: but to whom little is forgiven, the same loveth little. And he said unto her, Thy sins are forgiven. (Luke 7:36–48)

So much of His ministry is encapsulated in that one conversation: His ability to see the heart, the desires, of each individual; His abundant love for those who were repentant and recognized their Lord; His impatience with those who should have known better, to whom life had been very kind, but who were ungenerous and even cruel to those they saw as less than themselves.

Isn't it a fascinating statement, though, that Jesus links love to forgiveness?

Clearly, the overriding point of His teaching in this instance is to enlighten His host on the effect of His atoning sacrifice, which would occur shortly. In Gethsemane and on Golgotha, He performed the greatest act of love imaginable. The overwhelming gratitude we feel when it is revealed to us that we have been redeemed from our woundedness—even that which we have brought upon ourselves through poor choices or outright intransigence—transforms our hearts. It enlarges our tender, loving devotion to Him who did for us what we cannot do for ourselves. I understand and experience love for the Lord as a natural result of being a recipient of His freely offered forgiveness, and yet another reading of the concluding verse could be that our loving actions to others are the basis of our justification, His forgiveness. Not only are we commanded to love, love is the purpose of the plan of happiness and the means of participating in it. A better heart, then, is both the means and the result of turning to Christ.

I had a relative, a larger-than-life person in my younger years, who had a great zest for living and an instinctual generosity toward anyone in need. Like the Samaritan woman's, her life was complicated, and her relationship with the Church for most of her life was similarly knotty. She required her sons to attend church although she would seldom join them. She supported her sons and nephews and nieces on missions, though she stood in the parking lot or in waiting rooms during their temple marriages. She had a salty tongue and loved to shock (gently) her relatives with tales of her younger years. While she had a soft and unselfish way with nearly everyone else, she was a difficult mother.

She was the first person in my extended family to whom I confided that I am gay. I knew before I uttered the words that ungrudging acceptance and overwhelming love would be her instant response. For the rest of her years, she was for me a constant source of encouragement, an always available listening ear, an eager greeter of anyone who was important to me, an interested observer of my joys, and a constant consoler for any struggle.

One of my favorite stories about this splendid friend and relative occurred when one of her brothers was talking to her bishop. Her brother thought he was encouraging that bishop to come to know and care for his sister, who, the brother assumed, had not darkened chapel doors at any time during that bishop's tenure. Surprising the brother, this bishop revealed that he was very well acquainted with my relative; in fact, he considered himself in her debt for good works unselfishly and without fanfare performed. He told her brother that his sister paid tithing directly to Church headquarters, where it was then recorded in the local ward account. She apparently didn't want anyone nearby to know that she was a tithe payer. Perhaps it might have ruined some of her stories! Or, truer, I think, to the sincerity of her soul, she preferred not to receive recognition from any person on earth. All of her nieces and nephews loved to spend time with her, to be in her home, and to tag along on her various errands to help neighbors and others as she intuited a need. She accomplished those acts of quiet, normally unnoticed service with her trademark gusto and enormous good humor.

As she neared the end of her life, despite having engaged in a formal repentance process and made and kept temple covenants, she worried most what the Lord and her mother (who had died when my relative was a young teenager) would say to her when she met them. I have no doubt that the Savior sees in her a woman who developed a great capacity to care for others, whose unheralded and unceasing efforts lessened the load of many around her; she will certainly be the grateful and perhaps surprised beneficiary of His healing touch. I would love to witness as He says to her, "You have loved much; your sins are forgiven."

You likely know people like this as well. They are the ones I think Elder Jeffrey R. Holland had in mind when he shared, "Surely the thing God enjoys most about being God is the thrill of being merciful, especially to those who don't expect it and often feel they don't deserve it" ("The Laborers in the Vineyard," *Ensign*, May 2012).

I hope you feel yourself to be among the group Elder Holland described, a recipient of unexpected and unmerited grace.

And what of righteous deeds left undone? While not using thoughts of them as an opportunity to beat ourselves up, we occasionally perhaps ought to consider those opportunities we might have missed to bless the life of another. Why? In order to feel a stronger commitment to future action. Then-General Relief Society President Bonnie D. Parkin shared this experience of her daughter-in-law's mother, Susan:

> Susan was a wonderful seamstress. President [Spencer W.] Kimball lived in their ward. One Sunday, Susan noticed that he had a new suit. Her father had recently returned from a trip to New York and had brought her some exquisite silk fabric. Susan thought that fabric would make a handsome tie to go with President Kimball's new suit. So on Monday she made the tie. She wrapped it in tissue paper and walked up the block to President Kimball's home.
>
> On her way to the front door, she suddenly stopped and thought, "Who am I to make a tie for the prophet? He probably has plenty of them." Deciding she had made a mistake, she turned to leave.
>
> Just then Sister Kimball opened the front door and said, "Oh, Susan!"
>
> Stumbling all over herself, Susan said, "I saw President Kimball in his new suit on Sunday. Dad just brought me some silk from New York . . . and so I made him a tie."
>
> Before Susan could continue, Sister Kimball stopped her, took hold of her shoulders, and said: "Susan, never suppress a generous thought." ("Personal Ministry: Sacred and Precious," BYU Devotional, February 13, 2007)

As I remind myself of beneficial acts left unperformed and grieve over others' pain that I might have ameliorated or at least shared, I have wondered if Christ is ever disappointed in my rate of progress. It is fundamentally a pointless question, made moot both by His fore-knowledge and by His already provided forgiveness. Consequently, I have come to feel that the counsel of taking one day at a time reflects a divine principle. Rather than expending energy to review and regret, I can direct my zeal toward holier behavior and more righteous de-sires in the here and now. This is a sort of divine *carpe diem,* as dem-onstrated in the Lord's provision of daily manna to His people during their forty-year period of wandering (which was also their forty-year period of training and growing).

I believe the Savior looks liberally at our steps both forward and backward in our efforts to gain a better heart, one more aligned to our true and eternal nature, one shared with Him. Our reversions toward the shiny things of this world, despite our yearnings and de-sires for better, are known because "all things are present before [His] eyes" (Doctrine and Covenants 38:2). He sees our premortal as well as our postmortal selves and how small, daily efforts have molded our characters and our hearts, even on those days that to us are yet afar off. Periodically, we may need to remind ourselves that the second commandment is an injunction to love our neighbors *as ourselves.* Constant abasement, relentless self-criticism, and an ungracious ap-proach to ourselves is not of God and does not reflect obedience to that great commandment. Maybe this verse needs to be mounted to our morning mirror: "He that loveth not knoweth not God; for God is love" (1 John 4:8).

When we are overwhelmed, commandments can feel like bur-dens rather than expressions of His love for us and opportunities for us to put into action the love we have for Him. Being centered on the two great commandments can lessen those feelings we sometimes have that there are too many things to focus on. As Elder Dieter F. Uchtdorf said: "Our obedience to God's commandments comes as a natural outgrowth of our endless love and gratitude for the goodness of God. This form of genuine love and gratitude will miraculously merge our works with God's grace" ("The Gift of Grace," *Ensign*, May 2015).

I received a particularly meaningful email soon after *That We May Be One* was published, and I share a portion of it here as it relates to the nature of the virtuous cycle in which loving our neighbors more helps us to love our Lord more:

> Your encouragement and wisdom come in the nick of time for me—my son's wedding is next week. Try as I might I could not visualize me embracing his future husband and welcoming him into the family without being totally hypocritical. Now I feel the confirmation of the spirit that I can love them both and love my Savior at the same time. Indeed, I can love Him better as I learn to love them more. This is hard doctrine to learn and practice. (Name withheld, email to author, October 12, 2017)

The lesson this father learned had been modeled by my parents and their experience of learning to love more fully while increasing their faith. They did not find all the answers they would have wished about why their son was gay and what might be my place in the plan of happiness. But the revelation they did receive about their stewardship for their family was to erect no barriers to love or to my participation in all the family's activities and events.

Primary General President Joy D. Jones shared an experience that she and her husband had. They were feeling frustration over not being able to make a real connection with a couple who had not been to church in many years, but to whom they had been assigned to minister. She said they learned how to minister when their focus changed because of a scripture that spoke to them.

Here is the verse we read that changed both our hearts and our approach: "Thou shalt love the Lord thy God with all thy heart, with all thy might, mind, and strength; and in the name of Jesus Christ *thou shalt serve him*" (Doctrine and Covenants 59:5; emphasis added). Though this verse was so familiar, it seemed to speak to us in a new and important way.

We realized that we were sincerely striving to serve this family and to serve our bishop, but we had to ask ourselves if we were really serving out of love for the Lord. King Benjamin made clear this distinction when he stated, "Behold, I say unto you that because I said unto you that I had spent my days in your service, I do not desire to boast, for *I have only been in the service of God*" (Mosiah 2:16; emphasis added).

So whom was King Benjamin really serving? Heavenly Father and the Savior. Knowing the *who* and the *why* in serving others helps us understand that the highest manifestation of love is devotion to God.

As our focus gradually changed, so did our prayers. We began looking forward to our visits with this dear family because of our love for the Lord. We were doing it for Him. He made the struggle no longer a struggle. . . . We were worshipping and loving Him by loving His children. ("For Him," *Ensign*, November 2018; emphasis added)

Commandments are an indication of the Lord's love for us. They are both a symbolic and a concrete manifestation of His care for our pain, evidence of His keen yearning that we might spare ourselves and others wounds and sorrow. In Zenos's allegory of the olive trees (see Jacob 5), the Master repeatedly mourns when His desire to provide salvation has gone unrealized. As our hearts are changed, renewed, and bettered by love, His desolation at our previous distress, His anguish at prior unyielding, all such sorrows are replaced, tears dried, by joy at our turning, by exultation that we now love much.

PART THREE

THE GIFT OF CHARITY

CHAPTER NINE

WHAT IS THE GIFT OF CHARITY?

I know the color blue when I see it, and the flavor of a pear when I taste it;
I know an inch when I move my finger through it;
a second of time, when I feel it pass;
an effort of attention when I make it;
a difference between two things when I notice it;
but about the inner nature of these facts or what makes them what they are,
I can say nothing at all.
I cannot impart acquaintance with them to any one
who has not already made it himself.
I cannot describe them, make a blind man guess what blue is like. . . .
At most, I can say to my friends, Go to certain places and act in certain ways,
and these objects will probably come.

—William James, *The Principles of Psychology*, 2 vols. (1979), 1:224

As we consider Christ's love for each of us and ours for Him, our desires are multiplied to receive more consistently and in deeper measure the spiritual gift of His pure love, or charity.

Trying to describe the gift of charity with precision reminds me of a passage from Jane Austen's *Pride and Prejudice:* "I cannot fix on the hour, or the spot, or the look, or the words, which laid the foundation. It is too long ago. I was in the middle before I knew that I had begun." I feel the same way about trying to precisely quantify what constitutes the gift of charity, let alone delineate scrupulous steps necessary to qualify for it.

Do you recall the words that Paul used as he taught the citizens of Athens, those who lived in a city full of idols and loved to spend their time telling or listening to something new (see Acts 17:16, 21), but also those he perceived to be "most religious" in all things (Acts 17:22, footnote a)? As Paul spoke to them on Mars Hill, he taught them of their Heavenly Father using this expression:

> He also made all people of the human race to live over all the earth from one person, having determined beforehand their set times and the boundaries where they would live so that they might seek for God and perhaps feel for him and find him, although he is not far from each one of us. For we live in him and move and exist, even as some of your poets have said, "For we are also his offspring." Therefore, being the children of God, we should not think deity is like gold, silver, stone, or an image made by the skill and imagination of mankind. (Acts 17:26–29; in Thomas A. Wayment, *The New Testament: A Translation for Latter-day Saints*)

As I read these words, my sense is that Paul is trying to relate to the way his listeners might understand and approach God in the framework of their culture and knowledge. The phrase "perhaps feel for him and find him" encapsulates my experience with seeking to comprehend the doctrines of Christ's gospel as well as the process of becoming like Him. As I see it, the fulness of the gospel isn't offered to us as a recipe in a cookbook: do this in that measure, then the next thing in this way, and—voilà!—you will have your answer; you will have become perfected.

Unlike Paul or Alma the Younger, who seem to have learned of Christ with blinding insight in relatively short periods of time, for me, at least, that learning is a process of feeling after Him, wondering, pondering, praying, acting, and repenting as needed (daily!). That process is repeated over and over as I hopefully come closer to knowledge and wisdom.

I am intrigued by Paul's sensory metaphor, "feel for him." Likewise with the gift of charity, we cannot use our senses of sight, smell, taste, or hearing in order to pursue this capacity that we righteously desire. And *feel* in this sense is not to touch with our fingers; we cannot brush a divine attribute to calibrate and claim its quota, but we can feel *after* it. We can measure our own motivations. We can investigate the instinctive acts that have yielded illuminating insight in the past. We can act in faith on impulses, faint and deep as the call of a mourning dove, and evaluate end results.

Another way this "feeling after" has been described is as "knowledge by acquaintance" together with "knowledge by description" (these concepts are from Bertrand Russell's 1910 paper of the same title). We gain knowledge by acquaintance when we have an immediate awareness of a truth—for instance, when the Spirit testifies to our souls that Jesus is the Christ. On the other hand, knowledge by description is what we gain through inferential, mediated, or indirect means. An example of this latter sort of knowledge is to witness and test the fruits of truth, as Jesus invited His disciples (see Matthew 7:20). Both ways of increasing our knowledge of truth can be put to use as we seek to understand and gain the gift of charity.

I am fascinated that as Paul and Mormon each describe charity, they describe the company it keeps, and what it is not, perhaps because coming at it from both directions, as it were, might help us better comprehend and act.

	PAUL	MORMON
WHAT CHARITY IS	Companion to prophetic insight, understanding of mysteries, knowledge, and faith. Patient, kind, rejoices in truth. Bears, believes, hopes and endures all things. It is paramount among its companion virtues faith and hope. It is an eternal gift.	An essential characteristic in order to be acceptable before God, together with being meek and lowly in heart, and confessing by the power of the Holy Spirit that Jesus is the Christ. Long-suffering and kind, rejoices in truth. Bears, believes, hopes and endures all things. It never fails, and we are nothing without it. It is the pure love of Christ and endures forever.
WHAT CHARITY IS NOT	It is not jealous, boastful, arrogant, rude, or self-serving. It is not resentful or spiteful. It does not cease to exist after this life.	Is not puffed up, self-seeking, easily provoked. It is not evil-thinking and does not rejoice in iniquity.

When Paul begins his great sermon on charity, he does so by expressing its singular importance to one who would follow Christ:

> Though I speak with the tongues of men and of angels, and have not charity, I am become as sounding brass, or a tinkling cymbal.
>
> And though I have the gift of prophecy, and understand all

mysteries, and all knowledge; and though I have all faith, so that I could remove mountains, and have not charity, I am nothing.

And though I bestow all my goods to feed the poor, and though I give my body to be burned, and have not charity, it profiteth me nothing. (1 Corinthians 13:1–3)

As he concludes, Paul acknowledges that in this life our knowledge is incomplete, yet even when we are able to comprehend everything, charity will never fail:

For now we see through a glass, darkly; but then face to face: now I know in part; but then shall I know even as also I am known.

And now abideth faith, hope, charity, these three; but the greatest of these is charity. (1 Corinthians 13:12–13)

In his own treatise on faith, hope, and charity, Mormon links faith with hope, saying that without faith there can be no hope. Meekness, he teaches, is the necessary precondition that allows faith and hope to thrive in a person. Following on, he indicates that without charity we are nothing. He provides some attributes of charity that align well with Paul's teachings, including that it is the characteristic that never fails. Mormon then gives us this most precise and pithy definition of charity: "But charity is the pure love of Christ, and it endureth forever; and whoso is found possessed of it at the last day, it shall be well with him" (Moroni 7:47).

Mormon concludes his sermon with a plea for us to recognize the critical importance of the gift of charity:

Wherefore, my beloved brethren, pray unto the Father with all the energy of heart, that ye may be filled with this love, which

he hath bestowed upon all who are true followers of his Son,
Jesus Christ; that ye may become the sons of God; that when he
shall appear we shall be like him, for we shall see him as he is;
that we may have this hope; that we may be purified even as he
is pure. Amen. (Moroni 7:48)

What can we learn from these great prophets of the past?

Above all, faith is a necessary precursor to charity, because in order to gain the gift of charity we must first be followers of and be-
lievers in Christ. In a perfect virtuous circle, charity also increases
our faith. For example, think of a time when you have spent all day
helping some persons who might be strangers to you. You might have
been painting a house, clearing a long-neglected yard and planting
a garden, or perhaps building a school or digging a well. You might
have unraveled thorny school assignments, set up a new computer,
solved the conundrum of a stubbornly frozen smartphone. At the end
of your labors, how do you feel about these people, even if you do not
know them well? You feel a great love for them, you want them to be
happy because of the work you've performed, and you want their lives
to be better going forward than they have been in the past. And you
also feel grateful to your Heavenly Parents for having had this opportunity to do something that really matters, for allowing you to be an
instrument of Their love and peace. A heart that has been touched by
the experience of selfless service is a heart of gratitude and of faith, a
better heart than previously existed in that space.

In a revelation that the Prophet Joseph Smith called "the Lord's
message of peace to us," He provides specific virtues and attributes
that should accompany the Saints' preparations to build His temple.
The superlative element of righteousness, He identifies in this way:

"And above all things, clothe yourselves with the bond of charity, as with a mantle, which is the bond of perfectness and peace" (Doctrine and Covenants 88:125).

As we absorb these lessons, we may still be "feeling after" why charity seems to be the ultimate virtue and an eternal attribute. The most basic answer, to me, is that if we have not received the gift of charity, we have not become like Christ. Holiness is apparent in how we treat others, not in how eloquently we can speak of Him. We can repeat His words, we can know that He lives, we can even perform miracles in His name, but if we have not learned to love what He loves and in the way that He loves, we do not truly know who He is. Can we become like someone we don't know?

Another lesson from scripture and our own experience is that we come to know Him as we love and serve His Father, doing as He does. We come to know Him as we love and serve His people, all of the individuals who surround us. It is possible to do good works and donate large sums of money for people we don't love, and those works will benefit the world, yet there is no meekness in them. He loves with perfect knowledge of each individual. Although that will likely not be our constant blessing in this life, He is willing to share with us, when we diligently seek it, a sense of what He knows and values about specific people we encounter.

There has been a person in my life who I felt at one time had treated me quite poorly, had been unkind in a way that was very painful to me. I found it easy to maintain a cordial distance, to be polite and appear friendly while nursing and feeding my grudge, my own private little hoard of tarnished, bitter pennies. I didn't need to see this individual all that often, so the situation continued for a period of years, even during a time when I was making some financial contributions at this person's request (and, if I'm candid, feeling a little smug about it).

There came a moment, though, when I began to understand that failing to foster a genuine connection with this person had blocked better relationships with some others as a result. Around this same time, I learned something I had not known about a challenge this individual had faced earlier in life. I began to pray that I could let go of my hurt feelings and, more importantly, that I could feel love for this individual. After that, I was more open when we were together, and over time I came to recognize, in answer to those prayers, some sterling characteristics of this person that I had not before noticed. I began to see that some desires of this individual that I had mistakenly ascribed as seeking the praise of others were instead a genuine impulse to serve with creativity and enthusiasm. I came to admire and finally to love this person. I count the experience as a tender grace from a tender God.

That experience of coming to share Christ's pure love of that person changed my heart in a small way and made it better. If we think of the heart as the locus of love, it makes sense to think of charity as a lasting changing of our hearts so they become in the form and similitude of Christ's heart. An initial change to our hearts caused by our conversion to Christ may also make those hearts more available to the desire to learn His ways and His love. Our hearts become more expandable, more dynamic and vigorous, as our growing knowledge of His character embeds the yearning to diligently seek after this gift of charity. And continuing that process of seeking, knowing, learning, and loving is what makes the change in our hearts permanent.

The people of King Benjamin were immediately converted to Christ by the power of the Spirit accompanying his words, "And they all cried with one voice, saying: Yea, we believe all the words which thou hast spoken unto us; and also, we know of their surety and truth, because of the Spirit of the Lord Omnipotent, which has wrought a mighty change in us, or in our hearts, that we have no more disposition to do evil, but to do good continually" (Mosiah 5:2). Similarly, Alma related the impact the words spoken by Abinadi had upon his father, Alma:

> And according to his faith there was a mighty change wrought in his heart. Behold I say unto you that this is all true.
>
> And behold, he preached the word unto your fathers, and a mighty change was also wrought in their hearts, and they humbled themselves and put their trust in the true and living God. And behold, they were faithful until the end; therefore they were saved.
>
> And now behold, I ask of you, my brethren of the church, have ye spiritually been born of God? Have ye received his image in your countenances? Have ye experienced this mighty change in your hearts? (Alma 5:12–14)

It is the Lord's desire for us to have better, changed hearts. Charity is a gift He is eager to impart.

Ezekiel shares the Lord's promise: "A new heart also will I give you, and a new spirit will I put within you: and I will take away the stony heart out of your flesh, and I will give you an heart of flesh" (Ezekiel 36:26). That is His promise to us. As with all attributes in the divine nature, He will constantly beckon to us to share, He will always be aware of us, He will sustain and bless *as we turn to Him.*

The mighty change of heart, therefore, begins with meekness, a contrite and broken heart that allows space for Christ to heal and replace. The change continues as we daily act on our willingness to repent, having been baptized and confirmed, and as our desires and actions reflect an eagerness to follow and to please God, to give away our sins and to be sanctified of them, to do good continually, to endure to the end. In this lifelong process, as we constantly seek His gift of charity, it is almost as if our consistently better heart is finally molded by Him to pulse in synchrony with His own. We begin to feel what He feels in His love for His Father and for each person around us; we begin to see what He sees in the worth of every individual; we love what He loves and as He loves.

Another precondition of charity, and also its companion, is repentance. I sometimes think we make both too much and too little of Christ's gift to us of repentance. We make too much of it when we treat it as a process undertaken only for something so serious as to require a formal procedure that may include priesthood leaders. We make too little of it when we ignore the opportunities to make it an integral part of our learning process, and especially when we act as if it was simply a procedure to access at our convenience.

As President Russell M. Nelson has said, we will find added power when daily repentance is a consistent part of our lives:

> "Does *everyone* need to repent?" The answer is yes.
>
> Too many people consider repentance as punishment—something to be avoided except in the most serious circumstances. But this feeling of being penalized is engendered by Satan. He tries to block us from looking to Jesus Christ, who

stands with open arms, hoping and willing to heal, forgive, cleanse, strengthen, purify, and sanctify us. . . .

Nothing is more liberating, more ennobling, or more crucial to our individual progression than is a regular, daily focus on repentance. Repentance is not an event; it is a process. It is the key to happiness and peace of mind. ("We Can Do Better and Be Better," *Ensign*, May 2019; emphasis in original)

You will have your own examples of how regular repentance helps you to draw closer to the Lord. I find evening prayer to be a time to review my interactions with others throughout the day, to ask for His help to know what I could have done differently and better. I think we've all had the experience of knowing we haven't acted in the best, kindest, most loving way. In those settings, we sometimes rationalize our behavior by finding fault with the other person. We might look for excuses, like being too rushed, or too tired, or too preoccupied with something more important. Or we can identify our own shortcomings and ask the Lord to help us know how we can make that particular situation better and what we can do in general to avoid treating someone in that way in the future. Our repentance involves asking the individual's forgiveness as well as the Lord's, which deepens our learning process and helps strengthen our commitment to better future conduct.

A good friend once said she wants to win the gold medal in the repentance Olympics! I love that idea because it acknowledges that, fundamentally, repentance means turning to Christ. As we turn from difficult or simply unproductive learning and turn toward Him, we will always find things we can improve, and our Heavenly Father will always want to help us do so. When Jesus teaches us that His "yoke is easy, and [His] burden is light" (Matthew 11:30), I believe that He includes His portion of the repentance process—forgiveness—in that construct. He is eager to forgive. Indeed, as we think of His Atonement in Gethsemane and on Calvary's hill, we realize He has already given His part. As we sorrow for how we might have loved others better, as we ask His forgiveness and help in becoming more as He is, we feel His love in greater measure. I believe He loves our desires and actions to make use of His gift of Atonement.

In addition to repentance, a daily habit of gratitude centers our minds on the gifts and blessings the Lord has already abundantly provided. Former General Relief Society President Bonnie D. Parkin has observed:

> Gratitude is a Spirit-filled principle. It opens our minds to a universe permeated with the richness of a living God. Through it, we become spiritually aware of the wonder of the smallest things, which gladden our hearts with their messages of God's love. This grateful awareness heightens our sensitivity to divine direction. When we communicate gratitude, we can be filled with the Spirit and connected to those around us and the Lord. Gratitude inspires happiness and carries divine influence. ("Gratitude: A Path to Happiness," *Ensign*, May 2007)

You have experienced this truth: gratitude increases both our sense of love and our capacity to love.

As we count blessings each day, our minds are turned to the meaning and power of the spiritual gifts we have received. We can periodically review whether we are fully serving our brothers and sisters with these gifts before we seek additional capabilities. I am reminded of a story that my sister-in-law, Kathy Jacob Christofferson, shared at a BYU Women's Conference. I wish you could know her as I do! She is an extraordinary example of the kind of individual who thinks deeply about gospel topics, who diligently ponders and works out answers in her own mind before asking confirmation of the Lord, whose daily practices of repentance, gratitude, and prayerful desire to bring light to the lives of others has provided me with a better understanding of charity. Kathy said:

> When Elder Robert D. Hales was serving as mission president in the England London Mission, a young French sister missionary came to him seeking a blessing. She did not understand English when she was called to this mission, but she made it her goal to pray and study hard. She did make good progress for a time but then hit a plateau and didn't seem to progress any further. He laid his hands on her head to give her a blessing but then stopped. He received this revelation: he removed his hands and told her, "If you will thank the Lord for what you have already received, you will be able to progress further." She humbly followed this counsel and was able to progress rapidly in her fluency in English and became a wonderful missionary. ("By Small and Simple Things Are Great Things Brought to Pass," BYU Women's Conference address, May 3, 2019)

Making all of these practices a joyful part of our daily lives is an element of our larger learning process. As we accept callings and other opportunities to do His work, and as we seek to find those in need for whom we can be a source of aid, each experience provides a gift of further insight and inspiration. For example, after teaching a class, or speaking to a group, or acting as a ministering sister or brother, we can take some time to think about what went well and what could be improved. Both elements are important: what strengths can we continue to employ and what other things can become strengths? Such introspection is an act of optimism and an expression of gratitude for the ways the Lord allows us to serve in His kingdom.

Perhaps you have discovered, as I have, that when we identify a particular area in which we can incrementally improve our offering of service, making a specific commitment helps us be more focused on learning from the experience. Of course, I don't do this perfectly—there are times when I do things the old way, rather than the way I had pledged to do them—but over time, I find I'm getting at least somewhat better at it. I believe that's what the Lord is looking for from us: not perfect performance, but the desire to do His work more effectively, plus a willingness to keep trying. I think He wants us to find delight in the urge to be more effective in His service. Now, if you find this process to be negative or depressing, don't do it. What works for me may well not work for you. Find the ways that bring you closer to the Lord and help you feel His love as a result of being in His service.

Let me make a little digression to talk about discouragement, which might be described as self-disappointment. As President Ezra Taft Benson wrote: "We must be careful, as we seek to become more and more godlike, that we do not become discouraged and lose hope. Becoming Christlike is a lifetime pursuit and very often involves growth and change that is slow, almost imperceptible. . . . We must not lose hope. Hope is an anchor to the souls of men. . . . The Lord is pleased with every effort, even the tiny, daily ones in which we strive to be more like Him. Though we may see that we have far to go on the road to perfection, we must not give up hope" ("A Mighty Change of Heart," *Ensign,* October 1989).

The spiritual gift of hope in Christ is always linked to charity, and we require it in order to sustain the ongoing process of bettering our hearts. It will help encourage our hope, I find, if we think of perfection, our end goal, as it has been defined by Professor Frank F. Judd Jr.:

> The concept of perfection in . . . Old Testament references is not flawless behavior but rather a life of complete loyalty to Jehovah in spite of temptations and setbacks. . . . Significantly, [in the New Testament] the Savior indicates that a person does not achieve this type of perfection by simply keeping all the commandments. In the context of the story [of the rich young man], as an upstanding Jew who kept the Ten Commandments, the young man would have already likely made it a practice to give some of his wealth to those in need. But that past obedience was not enough to achieve perfection or completeness. The heart [or meaning] of perfection is true discipleship; it is following the Savior. ("'Be Ye Therefore Perfect': The Elusive Quest for Perfection," in *The Sermon on the Mount in Latter-day Scripture: The 39th Annual BYU Sidney B. Sperry Symposium* [2010], 125, 127)

And finally, as we progress in our efforts, having obtained the spiritual gift of charity, to retain it, Elder Dale G. Renlund provided additional insight into the process of moving forward after our hearts have been changed and made better, when he spoke of the characteristics of the lives of the people who had been converted by the preaching of the sons of Mosiah:

How did they successfully endure to the end? We know that they were "distinguished for their zeal towards God, and also towards men; for they were perfectly honest and upright in all things; and they were firm in the faith of Christ, even unto the end" [Alma 27:27].

Their zeal towards God likely reflects an eagerness to please God and worship Him with fervor and passion. Their zeal towards men suggests an ardent interest in helping and serving others. Being perfectly upright and honest in all things suggests that they held their covenants firmly and did not rationalize their commitments to God or man. We further know that they taught their children the gospel in their homes. We know that they buried their weapons of war, distancing themselves from temptations. ("Preserving the Heart's Mighty Change," *Ensign*, November 2009)

As I conclude this attempt to describe the godly gift of perfect love, I return to a formative experience I had as a young man, nearing the conclusion of my service in the Canada Montreal Mission. (I was not a very diligent journal keeper, which I regret, so my recollection here is likely imprecise and perhaps inaccurate in some details.) Sometime after the midpoint of my mission, I was serving in a gruelingly difficult area, Rivière-du-Loup, on the banks of the St. Lawrence. No one, from the mayor to the youngest child, was too busy to stop and heckle us as we rode by on our bikes, or as we were knocking on doors. The air was let out of our tires more than once. But I really loved the other elders in my zone and district as I served there, as well as the very few branch members and even fewer people who were willing to be taught. As you can gather, this area was not a real highlight of my mission.

Around that time, a friend in the mission office let me know I was going to be transferred. I am embarrassed to say that I entertained the hope that President Wayne Owens would call me as an assistant. (My admitting this may come as a surprise to some of my peers, whose faith would have wobbled had it actually occurred.) I had looked around at the other elders in the second half of their missions and immodestly figured I should be in his candidate pool. Proving I wasn't as advanced as I thought myself, when President Owens called an elder who in my un-humble opinion was rather "flashy" and not renowned for obedience to rules, I was taken aback.

Now, years later, I don't know what the Lord had in mind for that elder, or how his life has unfolded, but with the benefit of hindsight it is luminously clear to me the tutelage I was given. I was transferred to the Laval Zone, outside of Montréal. My companion was Elder Mark Messick from Salt Lake City. In those final months, in that marvelous companionship, I was granted a profound feeling of love for every sister and elder in that zone, receiving the gift of seeing them as Christ did. It was one of the sweetest and most sanctifying experiences of my life. I witnessed how the love we shared overflowed into the lives of the friends we were able to teach and baptize, to ward members and leaders, and in the letters we each sent home. What I initially considered a consolation prize for not being called to a more visible role was, without understatement, the highlight and even purpose of my mission, a gift given in spite of my pridefulness. I have learned many, many lessons in subsequent decades. One is to have compassion even on this earlier version of myself; another is to be constantly grateful that the Lord is endlessly patient with personal foibles and frailties, that He willingly works with inadequate instruments as He qualifies, shapes, and develops a heart, and a soul, for eternal growth, for His charity, which never faileth.

In the following chapters, I have attempted to describe some of the elements I have noticed in those whose lives reflect charity, in some way to share what I believe the gift of charity looks like "in real life." I hope these pages will generate additional ideas and inspiration as you pilot your own journey of discipleship. I gratefully testify that Jesus is the Christ, He is real, He lives, He is the Son of God, He died and was resurrected, He atoned for my sins and yours, He understands every pain and hope of my life and yours, He is my Friend and yours.

CHAPTER TEN

CHARITY INCREASES OUR FAITH BUT DOESN'T ANSWER EVERY QUESTION

Here let me pause, my quest forego;
Enough for me to feel and know
That He in whom the cause and end,
The past and future, meet and blend,—
Who, girt with his Immensities,
Our vast and star-hung system sees,
Small as the clustered Pleiades,—
Moves not alone the heavenly quires,
But waves the spring-time's grassy spires,
Guards not archangel feet alone,
But deigns to guide and keep my own;
Speaks not alone the words of fate
Which worlds destroy, and worlds create,
But whispers in my spirit's ear,
In tones of love, or warning fear,
A language none beside may hear.

—John Greenleaf Whittier, "Questions of Life"

Having been a commercial pilot in the early days of aviation, at the outset of World War II a French aristocrat joined the French Air Force, serving until his country's armistice with Germany. He was able to escape through Portugal to the United States, hoping to persuade the Americans to come to the aid of French and British allies. After a spending a little over two years in New York and Québec, he attached himself to an American convoy to Algiers so that he could join the Free French Air Force flying reconnaissance flights from North Africa and Sicily. In preparation for the Allied invasion of southern France, the aviator was assigned a mission to collect intelligence about German movements in the Rhone Valley. It was a mission from which he never returned.

While in North America, he wrote a children's book that has been translated into 300 languages and dialects, selling more than 140 million copies. The aviator was Antoine de Saint-Exupéry, and his book was *The Little Prince* ("Antoine de Saint-Exupéry," in *Wikipedia, The Free Encyclopedia;* https://en.wikipedia.org/w/index.php?title=Antoine_de_Saint-Exup%C3%A9ry&oldid=913022952; accessed September 5, 2019).

I initially loved the book in its English translation, and it was the first book I read in French, the language in which it was written. I served in the Canada Montreal Mission, and although I was called to a French-speaking mission, most of the time I spent there was in English-speaking areas. (When I'm asked if I've kept up on my mission language, I usually say that my restaurant French is well exercised; the rest, not so much.)

In the classic book, the Fox tells the Prince, "*Voici mon secret. Il est très simple: on ne voit bien qu'avec le cœur. L'essentiel est invisible pour les yeux*" (Antoine de Saint-Exupéry, *Le Petit Prince* [Paris, France: Editions Gallimard, 1946], 72). The passage is often translated into English as: "Here is my secret. It is very simple: It is only with the heart that one can see rightly; what is essential is invisible to the eye." Or, to put it in a way that relates to the topic at hand, even though our intellectual understanding may be cloudy, our spiritual feelings can be clear.

That's the formulation I would like to use in trying to describe how the gift of charity can increase the spiritual feelings that feed and grow our faith, even while we continue to move forward with questions our minds cannot fully answer.

The wonderfully insightful Sheri Dew has observed:

> Asking inspired questions leads to knowledge. It leads to revelation. It leads to greater faith. And it leads to peace. Not asking questions, on the other hand, closes off revelation, growth, learning, progression and the ministering of the Holy Ghost. . . .
>
> The Lord wants us to ask every probing question we can muster because not asking questions can be far more dangerous than asking them. Alma taught that those who harden their hearts receive less and less until they "*know nothing*. . . . And then they are taken captive by the devil, and led . . . down to destruction. Now this is what is mean by the chains of hell" (Alma 12:11; emphasis added). In other words, refusing to seek after truth makes you stupid. On the other hand, inspired questions asked in faith lead to truth—and "light and truth forsake that evil one" (Doctrine and Covenants 93:37). (*Worth the Wrestle*, [2017], 12–13)

A phrase that has often been used by members of the Church about thorny questions around doctrines, practices, or the history of the Church is "putting it on the shelf." The idea is that when we feel we cannot gain immediate answers, in times when we are spinning our intellectual wheels and finding no traction in identifying solutions or understanding, it can be better to put the question aside for a time. We might come back to it later with greater knowledge or spiritual insight. The metaphor of the shelf works for many.

In my life, I've found a metaphor that works better for me in my ongoing wrestle for answers and discernment. As I strive to fully comprehend the solution to thorny questions, I think of the ripples that appear on a pond when a stone has been thrown into it. The ripples closest to the stone's point of entry are the questions I am most engaged with right now, perhaps even constantly engaged. Moving out from the center, ripples represent other questions that I am occasionally considering, returning to them as new ideas come to me and I can bring fresh perspective. The farthest-out ripples are my cosmic questions, the answers to which I may never fully comprehend in this life. Retaining an awareness of those questions, even if they remain unanswered, helps me to keep periodic focus on the broadest part of my search for meaning and light.

As an example, I wrestle with an understanding of where I fit in the plan of happiness. I feel no desire to be sealed eternally to a woman. And yet I comprehend and delight that the highest degree of priesthood, the familial priesthood, is jointly held by a man and a woman, a union of opposites. I think of my parents and rejoice that exaltation requires a fusion such as theirs. I have many, many women friends whom I deeply admire, enjoy spending time with, and love, and I am delighted to imagine a next life in which these rich friendships continue endlessly. But the richest connection I have felt, the deepest love, was that shared with my former partner, who is male.

I have wondered how I can convey to you the love I have experienced. A soul after my own kind. Feeling known, the lumps and voids, the edges and center, by someone who sees me whole. Looking across a room for one face, and the simultaneous calming and private thrill of finding it. The weight and warmth of a gesture that imparts contentment and assurance. In a group, an eyebrow raised two millimeters that wordlessly speaks, "remember that time ten years ago?" bringing unvoiced laughter and private delight. Paragraphs spoken whole, alternating completion of thoughts, as well as companionable silence. A club with only two members, but one that shelters a roaring fire warming anyone nearby.

Yet, I have also learned through my life experiences not to tell the Lord there is something He can't do, or to contemplate that there could be something that I won't do for Him. So all I feel able to do is pray that if this—being sealed to a woman—is something the Lord wants me to do now, He will provide the attraction necessary to create and sustain a union that would be healthy and joyful for both partners. I am very aware that what we know about the next life is but a glimpse on the lip of the void, and so I try not to get too exercised about the details when the entirety of the big picture has yet to be revealed. But, at least for now, this struggle in my heart and mind stops my current progression in obtaining all available ordinances.

I don't think I'm alone in this particular wrestle. In addition to some of my LGBTQ brothers and sisters, I know straight men and women whose relationships or marriages have been so painful that they find it difficult to conceive of wanting to be sealed for the eternities. Left with such deep scars, they too currently pause at moving toward the highest ordinance of the temple.

So, on this question—the nature of eternal relationships—my intellectual understanding remains cloudy, but my spiritual feelings are clear: I know that my Heavenly Father loves me and that everything He does is good and for my good. Those spiritual feelings also help me to move toward answers at the margins of my broad question. For instance, I can reason that while the apparent focus of the God of the Hebrew Bible is on the productivity of relationships (as measured by conception of children), in some manner, this is another thing that is fulfilled and replaced by Jesus Christ's injunction to love our neighbors, including spouses, as ourselves. This line of thinking invites a focus on the quality of the relationship between spouses and brings substance to why Jesus teaches that adultery is such a grievous sin. I'm sure the full answer is richer and larger than what I am working out, but the direction in which my spiritual feelings lead me is one that is filled with love of and for God, and with increased gratitude for Christ and His gospel.

Of perhaps greater importance is that the waves of Spirit accompanying the desire for increased charity impel me to keep moving forward toward Christ, rather than remaining mired in what I cannot fully resolve.

I believe that one of the blessings in our lives as we act in charity is that we gain greater hope and faith in Christ, in His love for us as well as for all of His children. That faith enables us to avoid being paralyzed by unanswered questions, perhaps because the center of our attention has moved from ourselves to others.

It may also be useful, rather than constantly emphasizing what we don't currently know or understand, to consider what the outcome will be when we do know. By that I mean, how will I feel when I gain the additional light I am seeking? How will my faith be changed? How will my interactions with others be more holy? Considering this future state might change our present approach. I think of this in terms of tactics versus strategy, of journey versus destination. Rather than identifying to the Lord the specific answers we desire, we could plead rather for the anticipated outcome: a better heart, that our love might be a truer reflection of His. For some questions—such as mine about the plan of happiness—for which the answers seem unlikely to come in this life, such an approach can help us move to a point where the specific answer becomes less urgent, less necessary, because our overall understanding has significantly expanded.

I spoke at a forum some time ago in Salt Lake City with the stake president and bishop who had so kindly welcomed me to attend and participate in Church services and activities when neither my partner nor I were members. In that setting, a young person who struggled with many questions about being a gay Latter-day Saint asked how I dealt with questions like these: "Why am I gay?" "Did God do this to me?" "Am I really supposed to be alone through my whole life?" "Will I have the partner of my heart in the next life?" I wondered how best to respond, and in a flash of inspiration realized that for me something else had come to matter more. I said, "At a certain point I realized it was more important to know Him than to know why."

It was a moment of revelation to me, about me. I realized in that instant, with a clarity I had not before possessed, that I had indeed made the central question of my life how I could come to know Jesus so that I could truly follow and emulate Him.

Coming to know Him, as well as receiving answers to some of our most critical and complex questions, does not happen in an instant, in a day, or even in a year. We learn through both poor choices and rich blessings, through trials and errors, and especially through needed yet undeserved grace and mercy. Gaining this knowledge is the work of our existence.

Perhaps another useful metaphor for moving forward in faith while continuing to wrestle with challenging questions is that of a reservoir. Cities and towns construct reservoirs to store water in periods of prosperity in order that there will be sufficient for days of drought. In our spiritual reservoirs, we store light and knowledge already received, experiences with individual revelation of truth, the fruits of earlier struggles to gain clarity and peace. Those stored waters of faith and intelligence give us confidence to continue a current effort to come to grips with challenging doctrines, policies, or practices. What is already safeguarded in our spiritual storage gives conviction that we are proceeding in a positive direction even when we cannot clearly see the way forward. Because we willingly keep open minds and spirits, our devotional reservoir also is prepared to receive the additional waters of divine understanding we seek. "To those who have eyes to see and ears to hear, it is clear that the Father and the Son are giving away the secrets of the universe!" (Neal A. Maxwell, "Meek and Lowly," BYU Devotional, October 21, 1986). Studying, searching, pondering, and praying to gain revelation *because we have prepared room for additional knowledge and understanding* of the secrets for which we seek answers will yield treasures in the Lord's time and way. On the contrary, when we refuse the struggle, when we settle for easy, black-and-white, in-or-out answers, do we effectively declare our reservoirs full? Are we telling the Lord we have decided we know all we want to know?

The metaphor of a reservoir might also apply to our overarching desire to gain the spiritual gift of charity. We will need to drain unworthy desires, such as the need to be right, the need for others' approval, disdain for the poor who we feel have earned their plight, or a focus on the treasures of the earth, in order to make room in our spiritual basins for the pure love of Christ.

My frequent feeling, that I'm not yet perceiving all God is trying to show, helps me strive to see the Lord in each individual around me. I find divine light in expanded awareness of the lives and challenges of others. I gain enhanced empathy and a greater desire to do what I can to alleviate suffering. As the Reverend Dr. Martin Luther King Jr. put it: "We are caught in an inescapable network of mutuality, tied in a single garment of destiny. Whatever affects one directly affects all indirectly" ("Letter from a Birmingham Jail," http://okra.stanford.edu/transcription/document_images/undecided/630416-019.pdf).

We likely do not have a perfect understanding of the struggles of those around us, but rather than concentrating on what we do not know, we can make ourselves present and available to be with a brother or sister in need. And spending effort learning about and doing what we can to help improve the lives of others is likely to be far more fruitful in the end than continuing to spin our wheels about unanswered questions of the eternities.

I recall a particularly meaningful session of general conference on the morning of Easter Sunday, 2015. It seemed to me that the theme of each conference address related to our love for Jesus Christ and how we receive and understand His love by knowing His character and by serving in His name. Then-General Primary President Rosemary M. Wixom shared in a memorable address the story she had heard from a young mother who spoke in a ward Relief Society meeting of her journey of conversion—of reconversion, really. This young woman had wrestled with questions about her faith to which she could not find answers. Over a period of time, she received support from her family and ward members. They could not answer her questions, but they could and did love her throughout her process. President Wixom related:

> On that Sunday morning, as I listened to this young sister share the story of her journey, I was reminded that "it is upon the rock of our Redeemer" that we all must build our foundation [Helaman 5:12]. . . . During her lesson, I came to know more fervently that answers to our sincere questions come when we earnestly seek and when we live the commandments. I was reminded that our faith can reach beyond the limits of current reason.
>
> And, oh, how I wanted to be like those who surrounded this young mother, loving and supporting her. ("Returning to Faith," *Ensign*, May 2015)

With President Wixom, each of us can determine that we will surround with loving support those in our lives who struggle with their questions or their faith, just as the Lord bears us up in our own jostling for certainty. We can make room in our congregations for all spectrums of belief as we seek to "bear one another's burdens, that they may be light" (Mosiah 18:8). We need not have positions of influence in our ward or stake in order to make a unique difference in the life of another person. President Gordon B. Hinckley told of the impact one humble man has had in his determination to serve others:

I remember visiting a friend in southern India. . . . This man worked as an accountant in a cement plant. His salary was meager. His house was small; it would fit into the front room of many homes. But his heart was large and overflowing. Out of a great love for others that came from his understanding of the gospel of Jesus Christ, he built a school with his own hands on a piece of ground he bought from his savings. It was a simple rough building; but studying there were some four hundred poor children, each being brought out of the darkness of illiteracy into the light of learning. What this act of love has meant and will mean in their lives is beyond calculation.

Through this one man's efforts, there were established five small branches of the Church in the rural villages of southern India. The members constructed three or four little buildings, neat and clean. Over the door of each was a sign, in both English and Tamil, that read, "The Church of Jesus Christ of Latter-day Saints." The floors were of concrete and without benches where the people sat together as we met, shared our testimonies, and partook of the sacrament of the Lord's Supper. . . .

Some day, someone will write the story of the Church in India. That story will be incomplete unless there is a chapter on my friend who lost himself in the service of others. ("Whosoever Will Save His Life," *Ensign*, August 1982)

I share that story with a little trepidation: sometimes I fear that when we hear the stories of remarkable people, suddenly we see our own efforts and contributions as small, even meaningless. We need to constantly remember that the Lord does not give us charity in order to beat ourselves up, to make ourselves feel useless or incompetent. He gives the gift and also will tutor us in its use. He will open our spiritual eyes so that we can identify the moments and circumstances when He can use our particular efforts and abilities in His work of ministry to those who surround us. I hope we also remember that no effort to lift and aid another is unimportant. That effort is, in fact, essential as we develop in ourselves the character of Christ. In my own mind, I can imagine that good brother in India might not yet have gained certainty for all the questions in his life, and yet look at the impact he had by continuing to move forward in faith!

The Lord not only calls us as individuals to gain and act with His charity, He has the same expectation and requirement of His Church, composed entirely of imperfect individuals striving to become more like Him. This point was made by Elder Dieter F. Uchtdorf when he spoke to the missionaries of the Salt Lake City Inner City Mission in December 2015.

> We will not succeed if we only go through the motions of religiosity. We could cover the earth with members of the Church, put a meetinghouse on every corner, dot the land with temples, fill the earth with copies of the Book of Mormon, send missionaries to every country, and say millions of prayers. But if we neglect to grasp the core of the gospel message and fail to help those who suffer or turn away those who mourn, and if we do not remember to be charitable, we "are as [waste], which the refiners do cast out" (Alma 34:29). . . .
>
> To put it simply, having charity and caring for one another is not simply a good idea. It is not simply one more item in a seemingly infinite list of things we ought to consider doing. It is at the core of the gospel—an indispensable, essential, foundational element. Without this transformational work of caring for

our fellowmen, the Church is but a facade of the organization God intends for His people. Without charity and compassion, we are a mere shadow of who we are meant to be—both as individuals and as a Church. Without charity and compassion, we are neglecting our heritage and endangering our promise as children of God. No matter the outward appearance of our righteousness, if we look the other way when others are suffering, we cannot be justified. ("The Pattern, the Path and the Promise," transcript of address to the Salt Lake City Inner City Mission; http://newsroom.churchofjesuschrist.org/article/president -uchtdorf-transcript-salt-lake-inner-city-mission)

Those who serve in the Salt Lake City Inner City Mission are called to work with the homeless, with mentally and physically challenged individuals, with people living with addictions and many other kinds of difficulties. Most of the missionaries are senior couples who leave comfortable homes each day in order to work with those whose lives are in disarray. It is not easy work, and every day does not bring a feeling that their efforts have been effective. Rather, sometimes there is even a sense that their contribution is neither wanted nor valued by those they seek to serve.

Alma taught his people, "Nevertheless the Lord seeth fit to chasten his people; yea, he trieth their patience and their faith" (Mosiah 23:21). Sometimes that chastening can occur when our sincere and valiant efforts to help another are rejected or returned with unkindness. There is no greater example of this fact than Jesus's treatment at the hands of those who should have been His friends.

But we also find in Jesus's ministry a very profitable example of acting on current light while lacking complete understanding. During a trip to Israel, I visited the site of archeological remains of what is called the White Synagogue, on the shore of the Sea of Galilee in the ancient village of Capernaum. This synagogue was built in the third or fourth century AD. But underneath it lie the walls of an even older house of worship, which is believed to be the synagogue in which Christ preached the sermon we find recorded in the sixth chapter of John, wherein He speaks of Himself as the Bread of Life.

> I am the living bread which came down from heaven: if any man eat of this bread, he shall live for ever: and the bread that I will give is my flesh, which I will give for the life of the world. The Jews therefore strove among themselves, saying, How can this man give us his flesh to eat? Then Jesus said unto them, Verily, verily, I say unto you, Except ye eat the flesh of the Son of man, and drink his blood, ye have no life in you.
>
> Whoso eateth my flesh, and drinketh my blood, hath eternal life; and I will raise him up at the last day. For my flesh is meat indeed, and my blood is drink indeed. He that eateth my flesh, and drinketh my blood, dwelleth in me, and I in him. (John 6:51–56)

Hearing these words literally, many disciples found the Savior's teachings hard to hear and followed Him no more. "Many therefore of his disciples, when they had heard this, said, This is an hard saying; who can hear it? When Jesus knew in himself that his disciples murmured at it, he said unto them, Doth this offend you?" (John 6:60–61).

At this place in Capernaum, He turned to His Apostles and asked if they would also go away. Peter's words reflect his clarity: "And we believe and are sure that thou art that Christ, the Son of the living

God" (John 6:69). Although Peter may not have had all the answers, he knew the source of the answers he did have: that, indeed, Jesus was the Christ, the Son of the living God.

Like Peter, you and I can hold fast to what we now know and continue to walk in faith that additional light and knowledge will be forthcoming. We can decline to choose between our faith and our doubts, living according to the light we have already received as best we can, while trusting that the Lord will yet grant us more. We can daily seek the better heart that reassures us our urgent pleas for His gift of charity have been heard and are being answered with His daily manna to our souls. Our faith assures us that He has a longer and broader perspective. As the Perfect Judge of us all, He knows not only our actions but our desires, not only our questions but our faith. He knows the circumstances of our lives, how we have learned to think and choose, the chemistry of our consciousness and the biology of our bodies.

When we feel ourselves willing to continue moving forward in faith, it is an indication of the charity we have already gained—that we love truth, that we love the Giver of truth, even through a glass darkly.

CHAPTER ELEVEN

CHARITY REQUIRES INSPIRATION, NOT A DAILY LIST OF BOXES TO CHECK

*One of the profound privileges of membership
in The Church of Jesus Christ of Latter-day Saints
is that none of us have to take anyone else's word for what is true.
Personal revelation is a powerful, persuasive antidote
to uncertainty and confusion.*

—Sheri Dew, *Worth the Wrestle* (2017), 45

Moses's great desire, "Would God that all the Lord's people were prophets, and that the Lord would put his spirit upon them" (Numbers 11:29), can occur when we realize, as the Apostle John taught, "the testimony of Jesus is the spirit of prophecy" (Revelation 19:10). As the Lord's people, each of us can and should be prophets, armed with a firm testimony that Jesus lives, that we have felt His loving awareness of us, that we know His confirmation that our turning to Him, repentance, is welcomed and accepted. And with Joseph Smith, we can say, "I have learned for myself" (Joseph Smith—History 1:20). That is both the opportunity and requirement of discipleship as we seek to have our hearts changed to become more like His: through individual revelation we can be tutored through His Spirit.

Do you recall Alma's great dissertation on faith?

> But behold, if ye will awake and arouse your faculties, even to an experiment upon my words, and exercise a particle of faith, yea, even if ye can no more than desire to believe, let this desire work in you, even until ye believe in a manner that ye can give place for a portion of my words. (Alma 32:27)

We cannot simply be passive recipients of truth, we have to awake and arouse, then desire and experiment. It is true that to some is given the spiritual gift of belief on the words of another, "To some it is given by the Holy Ghost to know that Jesus Christ is the Son of God, and that he was crucified for the sins of the world. To others it is given to believe on their words, that they also might have eternal life if they *continue faithful*" (Doctrine and Covenants 46:13–14; emphasis added). My sense is that continuing faithfulness still requires us to awake, arouse, desire, and experiment, whether our spiritual gift is knowledge through the Holy Spirit or belief in the words of those who have gained their witness in this way. However we obtain it, we need to be actively engaged with the knowledge that has become the basis for our faith.

I am using the idea of a daily list of boxes to check as a framework for the opposite approach, one that relies on others for guidance and direction. We may be tempted to "crowdsource" steps of salvation, distilling them into a daily list of dos and don'ts. Charity, I have found, is lively rather than rote. It invites us to see all the shades of gray in the life of another, to discard comfortable, black-and-white ways of understanding the world. As an example, would we imagine that the Righteous Father of Two Sons went about his daily life as he always had while waiting for his younger son's return, or rather would we expect that he was seeking revelation to know how to handle this situation, how he could show his love to this most challenging child?

The German theologian and Christian martyr executed by the Nazis at Flossenbürg concentration camp in 1945, Dietrich Bonhoeffer, spoke of the challenge to Christians in the uniquely abominable circumstances of living in Nazi Germany. He called it the need to avoid retreating into a "private virtuousness":

> Such people neither steal, nor murder, nor commit adultery, but do good according to their abilities. But . . . they must close their eyes and ears to the injustice around them. Only at the cost of self-deception can they keep their private blamelessness clean from the stains of responsible action in the world. In all that they do, what they fail to do will not let them rest. They will either be destroyed by this unrest, or they will become the most hypocritical of all Pharisees. (In Eric Metaxas, *Bonhoeffer: Pastor, Martyr, Prophet, Spy* [2011], 470)

Gratefully, we do not face challenges of the same magnitude as Pastor Bonhoeffer and his contemporaries. But do we not also need to ensure that our efforts at personal piety, our desires to follow commandments and walk uprightly, do not end there? Are we also keenly aware of injustice around us and seeking divine guidance to know how we might act to make the world better?

As we think of the revelatory process associated with gaining charity, I think we could say that a passive focus on a checklist of "thou shalt" and "thou shalt not" is unlikely to develop the learning and experience essential for progression. The gospel of Jesus Christ cannot be lived through checklists because that gospel creates in us a desire to know Him, which knowledge will not come through passively expecting others to set our course. A checklist is an attempt to piggyback on someone else's experience and knowledge; it implies that the hard work of thinking and the trials of questioning and doubt will be accomplished by someone else, be it parent or prophet. If we will learn His true character and attributes, including and especially charity, we must build on what we have received through scripture, ancient and contemporary, by our own spiritual labor. We must incorporate our own experiments and desires to be divinely tutored. The five foolish maidens in Jesus's parable were in the right place at the right time—it would be accurate to say they were doing all the right things—but they were not prepared by the strength, faith, and conviction that come from having learned for themselves.

The risen Christ tells the people of the New World, "A commandment I give unto you that ye search these things diligently; for great are the words of Isaiah" (3 Nephi 23:1). I have come to love Isaiah, not least because of his glorious ability to write lyrical truth. In his great words, though, I find a requirement to engage my own faculties, to dig more deeply, to study and meditate, to seek enlightenment of the Holy Spirit. There are many books written to explicate Isaiah's words, and they contain helpful insights and historical context. But to know for myself what Isaiah teaches of Jehovah who will be born as Jesus, of Messiah and His millennial return, I must do my own work of preparing and engaging the Spirit of truth. Does it make sense to you, as you read some of his percipient phrases, that this is not the stuff of a list of dos and don'ts I can paste on my mirror?

For he shall grow up before him as a tender plant, and as a root out of a dry ground: he hath no form nor comeliness; and when we shall see him, there is no beauty that we should desire him. He is despised and rejected of men; a man of sorrows, and acquainted with grief: and we hid as it were our faces from him; he was despised, and we esteemed him not.

Surely he hath borne our griefs, and carried our sorrows: yet we did esteem him stricken, smitten of God, and afflicted. But he was wounded for our transgressions, he was bruised for our iniquities: the chastisement of our peace was upon him; and with his stripes we are healed.

All we like sheep have gone astray; we have turned every one to his own way; and the Lord hath laid on him the iniquity of us all. He was oppressed, and he was afflicted, yet he opened not his mouth: he is brought as a lamb to the slaughter, and as a sheep before her shearers is dumb, so he openeth not his mouth. He was taken from prison and from judgment: and who shall declare his generation? for he was cut off out of the land of the living: for the transgression of my people was he stricken. And he made his grave with the wicked, and with the rich in his death; because he had done no violence, neither was any deceit in his mouth. (Isaiah 53:2–9)

To fully absorb the divinity of Jesus Christ and His infinite Atonement, to know for ourselves that He is real and His doctrine true, requires an active engagement, an honest interrogation of our own souls, turning to Him, repenting, acting again with greater intention to know, seeking and receiving personal power to endure through Christ's enabling power and His witness to our minds and hearts of truth and needed action.

Failing to act to gain and grow this knowledge is like placing a beautifully wrapped gift in the middle of a table and admiring it day after day, enjoying its beauty, without ever opening and experiencing the gift.

So, how do we open the gift? How do we begin this process of actively engaging with the gospel of Jesus Christ? This has been a topic of many conversations I have had with a woman whom I am exceptionally fortunate to count as a friend and mentor, one who I believe has the spiritual gift of diligently seeking truth. We don't see one another often, but, for me, each discussion is illuminating. Professional and Church commitments fill my friend's calendar to overflowing, and yet she has learned the skill of being fully present in any given moment.

Both my friend and I have many opportunities to speak to and with young adults, and in those conversations, one topic that inevitably surfaces concerns gaining confidence in their ability to discern personal revelation from desires and ideas that are not the product of the Holy Spirit. We have felt a desire to help Latter-day Saints—particularly young adults—recognize that the feelings of the Spirit are not uniform across individuals. They can also vary within an individual's experience, depending on the specific need or topic.

On one occasion when we were discussing personal revelation, we remembered a general conference address delivered by Elder Richard G. Scott in 2009. Among other things, Elder Scott said:

> I am convinced that there is no simple formula or technique that would immediately allow you to master the ability to be guided by the voice of the Spirit. Our Father expects you to learn how to obtain that divine help by exercising faith in Him and His Holy Son, Jesus Christ. . . . I believe that you can leave the most precious, personal direction of the Spirit unheard because

you do not respond to, record, and apply the first promptings that come to you.

Impressions of the Spirit can come in response to urgent prayer or unsolicited when needed. Sometimes the Lord reveals truth to you when you are not actively seeking it, such as when you are in danger and do not know it. However, the Lord will not force you to learn. You must exercise your agency to authorize the Spirit to teach you. . . .

I bear witness that the Lord, through the Holy Ghost, can speak to your mind and heart. Sometimes the impressions are just general feelings. Sometimes the direction comes so clearly and so unmistakably that it can be written down like spiritual dictation. ("To Acquire Spiritual Guidance," *Ensign*, November 2009)

I stated my concern that the phrase *spiritual dictation* used out of context could suggest that receiving personal revelation was a somewhat passive process. That would belie the intensive work and effort that go into being prepared to receive revelation, seeking it, recording it, and trying to understand as clearly as possible what the Spirit is communicating. In particular, I said I was concerned that young adults could get the impression that if they weren't receiving "dictation," they weren't receiving revelation. My wise friend pointed out what we both already knew: that the Spirit conveys insights to us in ways we learn best, that a given situation may require a variation in the method of revelatory delivery, and that the best way to gain confidence in the source of feelings and ideas is through personal effort, which at least at the outset involves trial and error.

Do you remember the movie *Groundhog Day*, featuring Bill

Murray and Andie MacDowell? In a delightful and wise comedy, the lead character lives the same day over and over and over. Regardless of what he does, even trying to kill himself, the same Groundhog Day begins again each morning. But he finally learns, through trial and error, to spend his time and efforts in perfectly serving all the people around him. Once he has learned to live his life to benefit others, a new day finally dawns. Aren't we rather like this character, as our own trials, errors, and victories often provide a way of learning through both negative and positive experiences?

Going back to my conversation with my friend: she also suggested we should teach that the facility to regularly receive revelation as clear as "spiritual dictation" requires two things: a lifetime of effort to purify ourselves, and the Lord's desire in a given moment to be quite specific, rather than leaving us to work out the details, as He most often does. For example, when President Russell M. Nelson speaks of the pace and volume of spiritual direction he receives, we should recognize that he has diligently devoted enormous effort over decades to honing his ability to consume what the Lord would offer. Young adults especially neither need to be disappointed that their skills in this area are not equal to his, nor to deprecate his description of a revelatory process simply because it is not congruent with their current experiences.

President Nelson has said: "One of the things the Spirit has repeatedly impressed upon my mind since my new calling as President of the Church is how willing the Lord is to reveal His mind and will. The privilege of receiving revelation is one of the greatest gifts of God to His children" ("Revelation for the Church, Revelation for Our Lives," *Ensign*, May 2018).

Prophets, ancient and modern, have provided examples of receiving revelation through the experience of "pure intelligence," through feelings, such as the "burning in the bosom" referred to in Doctrine and Covenants 9:8, feelings of warmth and comfort, and through a voice in the mind. And, of course, there are other ways, such as dreams and visions. President Boyd K. Packer said, "The seventh chapter of Moroni in the Book of Mormon tells you how to test spiritual promptings. Read it carefully—over and over. By trial, and some error, you will learn to heed these promptings" ("Personal Revelation: The Gift, the Test, and the Promise," *Ensign*, November 1994).

To bring this discussion back more specifically to our desires for a better heart, in my experience, one way to become more familiar with how the Spirit communicates with you—to learn by trial and error—is to focus on your desire to serve others. As you pray each morning that the Spirit will help you identify opportunities to serve, you will learn to follow impulses to do good. Because of the frequency with which these opportunities to serve can arise, you will begin to distinguish between what comes from within you and what comes from beyond you. Combined with daily immersion in the scriptures and continued prayer, serving will help you become more confident both in the Lord's personal knowledge of you and in how He guides you through His Spirit.

As we work and pray for the gift of charity, we will receive revelation teaching us how to act in ways that sustain and grow the gift. It is an expansive way to exist in the world, recognizing that we have already been given personal gifts of the Spirit and talents that communally nourish a family, a neighborhood, and the Church as the body of Christ. But that munificent impact would be blunted by a tendency to treat this connection with heaven as if we expected the Lord to give us a detailed to-do list every morning. His power is in us, if we will but use it, to be agents who act. Then we will be given further tutoring as to *how* we can act in love for Him and for our neighbors.

We consider the aim of our efforts to be having our hearts changed by charity, the pure love of Christ. Our focus is on who we are becoming—indeed, on Whose we are becoming—rather than the tactics of the learning process. When our primary object in life is to *love* perfectly—to persistently and consistently seek the gift of charity—then we may discover all the Savior was striving to teach us about contrite and ultimately changed hearts: "By this shall all men know that ye are my disciples, if ye have love one to another" (John 13:35).

When we seek to love perfectly, our focus is outward. We strive to learn what it is that God loves about each one of His children. Knowledge of our own shortcomings creates a humble desire to aid, to lift, to serve a brother or sister in need.

Jesus's encounter with the rich young ruler may be an example of seeking external performances to validate our inward feelings of personal righteousness. Have you ever wondered how this young man thought Jesus would answer his question, "what lack I yet?" (Matthew 19:20).

Since his youth, he had kept the commandments Jesus enumerated. Did he expect Jesus would provide another commandment or two? Perhaps he thought he would be tasked with an errand or even a foreign mission? Mark tells us that "Jesus beholding him loved him" (Mark 10:21)—we sense his desires are good and pure, that he is indeed a worthy, dutiful young person who has been carefully obedient his whole life. Possibly now he was seeking an additional list of performances to certify to himself his worthiness, misunderstanding that the gospel of Jesus Christ seeks to change our actions, predominantly as a means to change our hearts.

As Bishop Gérald Caussé so astutely asked: "My dear brothers and sisters, are we active in the gospel, or are we merely busy in the Church? The key is to follow the example of the Savior in all things. If we do that, we will naturally focus on saving individuals rather than performing tasks and implementing programs" ("It Is All about People," *Ensign*, May 2018).

I hope this doesn't sound dispiriting or discouraging. Our perfect Savior knows that we are not perfect, nor is His expectation that we will be complete in this life. Rather, it is our desires and efforts to improve that please Him.

As President Russell M. Nelson wisely advised:

> Meanwhile, brothers and sisters, let us do the best we can and try to improve each day. When our imperfections appear, we can keep trying to correct them. We can be more forgiving of flaws in ourselves and among those we love. We can be comforted and forbearing. The Lord taught, "Ye are not able to abide the presence of God now . . . ; wherefore, continue in patience until ye are perfected" (Doctrine and Covenants 67:13).
>
> We need not be dismayed if our earnest efforts toward perfection now seem so arduous and endless. Perfection is pending. ("Perfection Pending," *Ensign*, November 1995)

Where we are in our lives and what improvement means are matters solely between Him and ourselves. No one else can or ought to give us the answer to such questions. And this is another area in which our daily prayer to find opportunities to serve Him is beneficial: service necessarily takes us outside ourselves because our attention is on others. In this effort, we care more about what someone else is experiencing than about our own wants and desires. We consider both Whom we worship and what we can do to convert adoration into action.

We can also resolve that we will be unwilling to be offended. To be in control of our own responses to others means that we have the power to destroy enemies—because we resist considering or counting any individual in that category in our lives.

I'm reminded of a story told of Benjamin Franklin. Apparently, there was a man in Franklin's circle with whom he found it difficult to get along. Franklin was aware that this man had an extensive library of which he was proud, so he asked to borrow a book. The man agreed, and, in a short period of time, Franklin returned the book together with a gracious note of appreciation. On the strength of that transaction, a friendship was born (see "Ben Franklin effect," in *Wikipedia, The Free Encyclopedia;* https://en.wikipedia.org/w/index.php?title=Ben_Franklin_effect&oldid=895799762; accessed September 3, 2019).

As we seek revealed opportunities to serve others, we might likewise consider that allowing them to help us is also an act of service, and our gratitude can link our hearts with theirs.

Oh, how great the goodness of our God, that He not only allows us to play a role in His work but also leads, teaches, and inspires us as to how we can!

To wrap up our discussion of inspired direction, here are some examples in the lives of people I admire who received callings without specific guidance as to how they were meant to accomplish the desired result. They could not rely on checklists—there weren't any—rather, their only way to serve was to gain revelation.

The Avenues area of downtown Salt Lake City is lovely and historic. Homes on these beautiful, tree-lined streets were built by Latter-day Saint pioneers and their children. Over the intervening decades, these homes where eight and ten children had been raised were deemed too small for a family with two or three children, and the proximity of the area to the university made it desirable for singles living together, newlyweds, professors, and staff, among others. Today, the population of Latter-day Saints in the Avenues is likely lower than 30 percent. But over the years a feeling had grown among some residents that their Latter-day Saint neighbors were cliquish and socialized only with each other. A number of members were asked by an insightful leader to create a Fourth of July event that all neighbors might join, so that friendships could expand between Church members and their neighbors. By the time I lived in the area, they had developed a formula for an event that an entire neighborhood had come to embrace. They made the decision to hold the event on the street near the chapel, rather than inside it—close enough to move chairs and tables but on "neutral" ground. They delivered invitations to every house, and the first item printed under "Menu" was coffee. In this situation, it was the perfect way to show an outstretched hand. And when the Emigration Stake was assigned to build a float for the Days of '47 parade, the decision was made to create a neighborhood float rather than one solely representing the stake. Friendships were built among people constructing the float, both stake members and neighbors rode on the float, and specific neighborhood homes were depicted. At a sacrament meeting soon after, three neighbors who do not belong to our Church were invited to speak and share their feelings about the experience. Where once there was a feeling of exclusivity, inspired Church members and leaders have found their own ways to act to create inclusion.

In another case, a very successful professional and his wife, at an age when they might have been considered "emeritus," were thrilled when he was called to be bishop of a newly created mid-singles ward. Rather than filling these years with trips exploring the world or enjoying vacation homes, this couple dived headfirst into creating a loving, welcoming environment in this new ward. Recognizing a primary need to build social connectivity among the ward members, they were inspired to call one-third of the ward members as missionaries to work with the full-time sisters assigned to the ward, to take the good news of the gospel to peers, both investigators and less-active members of the Church. Home evenings and other events for the ward include both social activities and learning opportunities. A sweet spirit of acceptance and kindness is evident among the members of the ward, and they revere their bishop and his wife for the generosity with which they give their time, their means, and above all their loving care.

Another couple has served for a number of years on a regional public affairs committee, with a special focus on interfaith outreach. They were given broad latitude as to how to accomplish their mandate, left to gain revelation on what to do to move forward. They joined an existing interfaith group in the city, and from there on their focus was on building individual friendships with leaders and members of other congregations. They found much to admire in their new friends, and they eagerly joined in multifaith efforts to deal with local issues. Over a number of years, theirs have become familiar faces in many different churches in the area. They helped a local church gain permission to use a Latter-day Saint building for a period when their sanctuary was damaged by fire. They are sometimes asked to speak to other faith groups, and they work to provide opportunities for leaders of other faiths to meet leaders of our Church and to come to know its members. Hearts and minds that once were closed, on both sides, have opened with expanded understanding and love. Bridges of love have been built, and, on more than one occasion, I have heard this couple welcomed from a pulpit with the words, "We are so glad to welcome our friends, who represent our sister church, The Church of Jesus Christ of Latter-day Saints!"

You will find in your own life examples of those who seek and receive inspiration in their callings—official and self-identified—to lift burdens, to build bridges, and to do the Lord's work in His way. My hope is that each of us will gain greater facility in divinely sourced communication so that our hearts will also be more refined, more like His.

CHAPTER TWELVE

CHARITY MAKES US A CONDUIT OF CHRIST'S LOVE, EVEN WHILE WE ARE YET IMPERFECT

Who am I to judge another
When I walk imperfectly?
In the quiet heart is hidden
Sorrow that the eye can't see.
Who am I to judge another? . . .

I would be my brother's keeper;
I would learn the healer's art.
To the wounded and the weary
I would show a gentle heart.
I would be my brother's keeper—

—Susan Evans McCloud, "Lord, I Would Follow Thee" (*Hymns*, no. 220)

In my career, I have had responsibility for sales and marketing organizations. Our clients were institutional, rather than retail buyers of our services, so the model for our engagement with them was "business to business" rather than "business to consumer." But the insight one quickly gains is that even when a potential client is a business, the decision makers, the buyers, are individual consumers. The most powerful ways to communicate our messages, then, required an understanding of each buyer's concerns and hopes, their motivation and purposes. So, even though we were engaging with other businesses, our focus was more akin to focusing on retail consumers. Does this remind you of the truth that the Lord has concern for the entire human family, and yet His focus is on each one of us as individuals?

In marketing we paid some attention to the concept of generational cohorts. Setting aside the obvious flaws inherent in generalizations, you might have found in your own experience that, particularly for those born after 1970, there is an almost inborn instinct for fairness as a motivating value. It is a wonderful attribute, and although there is much yet to be done, many of the benefits of our world are more widely accessible than ever before, inherited privilege carries less power, and ubiquitous social media magnifies individual voices.

And yet, as we think of these concepts in a spiritual way, fairness is the hallmark of justice, while mercy is inherently unfair. It is unfair that Christ suffered all pain, afflictions, illness, and temptations so that I might not, if I choose, fully bear the required consequences of my choices. To state it in another way, Lucifer's plan was entirely fair (albeit contrary to the eternal law of agency, and therefore unenforceable), Christ's plan completely unfair. The plan of salvation allows me to suffer in order that I might learn and grow, but the most acute, the most horrific suffering has already been endured by my Savior, and this He has done to spare me from what I merit and deserve.

In 1908, a thirteen-year-old boy by the name of George Archer-Shee was a cadet at the Royal Naval College, Osborne, in England on the Isle of Wight. He was accused of having stolen and cashed a postal order, resulting in his dismissal from college and thus from the Royal

Navy. The consequences of such a charge would have had significant ramifications, both personal and social, for the boy and his family. George's father and brothers were socially prominent bankers, and the charge against him, as well as his public dismissal from the navy, would have caused reputational damage and social approbation for the entire family. More important, though, the family were devout Roman Catholics, and the charge implicated their moral principles. Because the Royal Navy, considered part of the British Crown, had reached a formal decision, the only way to overturn their verdict was to seek a Petition of Right. The Crown cannot be sued in civil court, so the doctrine of *fiat justitia,* "let right be done," was developed. Upon approval of the Home Secretary and Attorney General that a case qualified under the doctrine, it could be heard in court. Those defending Archer-Shee gained that approval, and, in the end, the Crown agreed that the boy had been truthful; he was not a thief.

The Archer-Shee case was the factual basis for a fictionalized account in a 1946 play by Terrence Rattigan called *The Winslow Boy,* made into a film in 1948. In 1999, David Mamet wrote a screenplay and directed a new film, also called *The Winslow Boy.* It is a favorite of mine, and at the conclusion the character played by Jeremy Northam, the barrister for young Winslow in his case against the Crown, after having won the case, says, "It's easy to do justice, very hard to do right."

As we think of our Savior's gift of charity, then, we can accurately consider that we are praying for an expanded ability to also be unfair in order to do right: to free others from the justice they deserve in any hurt or offense they have caused us by our freely offered, unconditional forgiveness. We are seeking to replace grudges with grace, unkindness with unearned love. Perhaps that is why Christ is willing to share a divine attribute and characteristic with imperfect individuals: because our desire to gain it is solely to serve and bless others.

As the Apostle Paul wrote to his brothers and sisters in the Roman Church: "For all have sinned, and come short of the glory of God; Being justified freely by his grace through the redemption that is in Christ Jesus" (Romans 3:23–24).

I have earlier described the interaction of the Samaritan woman with Jesus at Jacob's Well. She is a powerful example of the goodness of the ordinary people who surround us. They are as imperfect as we are, and yet, when they are given the opportunity to recognize and identify grace through the redemption in Christ, their true magnificence becomes apparent. Perhaps we can remember, as we have the blessing to work with people whose lives are not all they would hope, that our invitation to repentance will be less impactful without our personal witness of experience with His loving grace.

As author Camille Fronk Olson has observed about the Samaritan woman's experience: "Jesus did not commence the conversation by pointing out what the woman needed to change in order to recognize and follow him. Rather, he began by opening her eyes to possibilities that exceeded anything she could have imagined" (*Women of the New Testament* [2014], 222).

When she recognizes the promised Messiah, her entire aim becomes helping others to gain the same priceless understanding she has found. Christ's earthly mission was to the tribe of Judah, and yet the great desire and belief evidenced by this community of Samaritans—sparked by one very human and therefore flawed individual—caused Him to remain two days teaching and blessing these people, considered Gentiles.

Though she was not present to hear the lawyer's question, this woman understood the two great commandments, to love her God and her neighbors. She did not constrain herself, feeling that if she couldn't keep every obligation and performance of the law, she would keep none. Rather, she did what she could in her circumstances—and what she could do was to share the news of Jesus, the Christ, the long-awaited and promised Messiah, even with the very people likely to have shunned and treated her poorly. She was to them, certainly, a conduit of their Savior's love.

I find great comfort in those verses, and recognition that the Lord can use me in spite of my shortcomings and weaknesses. I rejoice that in His complete knowledge of the whole of me, I also find perfect love.

As you and I strive to become disciples, is there in the deepest recesses of our souls a nagging thought that God will only work with people closer to perfection than we are at that moment? Do we harbor an inarticulate preoccupation that we are not now, and never will be, quite good enough to be worth His attention and love? And yet, can we imagine that there is any element of our hearts, our minds, our souls, that the Lord does not know completely? Our theology suggests that Jesus experienced every element we assess as unworthy about ourselves—He knows, and still He loves.

So, as we experience His love, we can free ourselves from the effort of trying to appear that we (or our children) are something other, better somehow, than who we really are. As we do so, we free ourselves to be more open to others, less prone to envy, more susceptible to empathy. We become more able to receive the gift of seeing and loving as our Redeemer sees and loves.

I have come to believe that the greatest power of godliness is love, that the purpose of everything the Father and Son do stems from their unstinting, unqualified, unending love. Can there be a greater proof of the power of that love than the willing Atonement and Resurrection of the One perfect person ever to walk on this earth? I believe the most meaningful trials of our lives are trials of love: when we are in doubt or pain, will we choose God above all (as He chooses us)? When we are battered by actions or inactions of others, will we still choose to love them?

Occasionally in a Sunday School class, some variation of this question will come up: "How do we reconcile the first and second great commandments when they are in conflict?" It always generates discussion, and perhaps that's the point of asking it, but I think it represents a false duality, an inaccurate understanding. Another variant of the theme is the well-meaning but impossible advice to "focus on loving God first, and when you've mastered that, then add loving neighbors to your efforts." Is it even possible to love God and not love what He most loves, His family? The effect of loving only neighbors without concurrently loving the Creator can produce beneficial effects in the community and world, but it lacks the crucial uplift of seeing the eternal possibilities, the infinite potential, of each individual. Loving God helps us to see what is godlike in our neighbors; loving those around us helps us to understand the eternal purposes of God. We cannot fully live either great commandment in isolation, we can only honor God as we bless His children.

A dear friend who returned to activity in the Church about the same time as I did, and in the same ward, shared with me an experience she and her family had while undertaking a service project in Central America. Her husband is not a member of our Church and has been wary of efforts of ward members or missionaries to befriend him. When I lived in the same community, his practice was to attend sacrament meeting with his wife and daughters and then take the girls with him to worship in the church that he attended. He was hypersensitive to messages he felt his daughters were receiving in our meetings about doctrine and truth.

The service project that this family joined was organized by some members of our Church, and most of the participants were Latter-day Saints. This husband was immediately on his guard about how their time would be spent and with whom. But over the course of days, as he joined in hard work to make the lives of local people better, he came to relax and enjoy the friendship offered by other participants in the project. My friend told me how people went out of their way to include her husband, to extend friendship without talking about the Church, simply trying to get to know him. She said for him this was a powerful experience of being able to see members of The Church of Jesus Christ of Latter-day Saints as people who were willing to sacrifice their time and money in order to help others, who made no judgments about him but always made him feel included, who were interested to hear his beliefs, if he wanted to share them, without feeling the need to challenge or correct. "They just listened!" said my friend. "And they asked questions and listened some more. They laughed together and they did hard things together, and somehow as the days went by his defenses started to come down. By the end, he could acknowledge the goodness he saw in this group of people who were simply trying to be like Jesus."

This good man didn't suddenly decide he wanted to join the

Church, but this experience did make a difference in his willingness to support his wife in her activity in it.

I sometimes think our attention, as we try to share the love for and from Christ that we feel, ought to be oriented simply toward expanding friendships rather than adding converts. We can look for the wonderful attributes and characteristics others possess; we can enjoy coming to know them and letting them know us. Our metric of success in these endeavors ought not to be whether someone joins our Church, but whether we have been able to give and receive pure love. We can, rightly, leave conversion to the Holy Spirit.

Elder Robert C. Gay taught this lesson in an unforgettable way:

> A few years ago my older sister passed away. She had a challenging life. She struggled with the gospel and was never really active. Her husband abandoned their marriage and left her with four young children to raise. On the evening of her passing, in a room with her children present, I gave her a blessing to peacefully return home. At that moment I realized I had too often defined my sister's life in terms of her trials and inactivity. As I placed my hands on her head that evening, I received a severe rebuke from the Spirit. I was made acutely aware of her goodness and allowed to see her as God saw her—not as someone who struggled with the gospel and life but as someone who had to deal with difficult issues I did not have. I saw her as a magnificent mother who, despite great obstacles, had raised four beautiful, amazing children. I saw her as the friend to our mother who took time to watch over and be a companion to her after our father passed away.
>
> During that final evening with my sister, I believe God was asking me, "Can't you see that everyone around you is a sacred

being?" ("Taking upon Ourselves the Name of Jesus Christ," *Ensign*, November 2018)

Think about Alma's description of the covenants that we make at baptism: "And now, as ye are desirous to come into the fold of God, and to be called his people, and are willing to bear one another's burdens, that they may be light; Yea, and are willing to mourn with those that mourn; yea, and comfort those that stand in need of comfort, and to stand as witnesses of God at all times and in all things, and in all places that ye may be in, even until death, that ye may be redeemed of God" (Mosiah 18:8–9). That really is a call for us to be in community with one another. In that sense, we cannot fulfill our covenant by ourselves—we need to be fully engaged with others. The gift of charity, likewise, changes our hearts, but it does so as we work with, pray and care for, serve, hold, encourage, lift, and love those around us.

I have a wonderful memory of an extraordinary evening of celebration and love. Very dear friends of mine, including Darius Gray, Tamu Smith, and Zandra Vranes, had been part of a committee charged with creating an event to celebrate the fortieth anniversary of the long-hoped-for revelation on priesthood and temple given to President Spencer W. Kimball that acknowledged the Lord's desire that Black members of the Church should have access to every ordinance, blessing, and opportunity to serve. The result of the efforts of that committee, and of many other individuals and Church departments, was "Be One: A Celebration of the Revelation on Priesthood." Sister Gladys Knight had organized the spectacular Be One Choir, which brought a spirit and rhythm to the Conference Center I had not before experienced there. The wonderful Bonner Family stole the hearts of all who heard them, Alex Boyé performed, and narrators, singers, and dancers told the stories of Black Latter-day Saint pioneers in many nations.

That evening in June 2018 reminded me that on June 9, 1978, I had been a missionary serving in Montreal, Québec. My companion and I had gone to the mission office to pick up some materials and heard that the Church had just announced the revelation extending full priesthood and temple participation to our Black brothers and sisters. We were all overjoyed, and I used one of the office phones to place a (collect) call to my parents to tell them the good news. We immediately left to tell what God had revealed to His prophets to a wonderful man we were teaching who had immigrated to Canada from Haiti.

In subsequent years, I had been interested in reading what histories I could find about individuals who had joined the Church knowing that, due to an immutable part of themselves, their genealogical ties to Africa, they would not be able to participate in the same ways as others.

Some thirty years after my missionary service, I had the opportunity to meet Darius Gray, who served in the original presidency of the Genesis Group, a quasi-branch of the Church whose organization was approved by Elders Gordon B. Hinckley, Thomas S. Monson, and Boyd K. Packer, all then serving in the Quorum of the Twelve Apostles. As I returned to activity but not yet membership in the Church, I was thrilled to be able to talk to Darius about his experiences both before and after the 1978 revelation. I remember telling him that I was in awe of his faith in remaining active in the Church through all the years between his baptism in the early 1960s and the announcement of the revelation. He replied, "I wasn't!" He talked about the challenges he had faced and the times when he had felt he could take no more and temporarily distanced himself. I leave it to Darius to tell his own story, but he is, to me, a great example of kindness and humility, of one who has repeatedly turned the other cheek not by necessity but by choice. I consider him both mentor and personal hero.

That summer 2018 evening in the Conference Center, seeing Darius and other friends sitting on the stand was thrilling to me. I was so grateful that both they and I had lived to see this moment of grateful joy and celebration. I wondered if this commemoration acknowledging our expanded understanding of God's love for all of His children might have been similar to how the original membership of Christ's Church and their Gentile brothers and sisters in a conference must have felt:

> Then Peter began to open his mouth and say, "I truly understand that God does not show partiality. But in all nations, anyone who fears him and does what is right is acceptable to him."
>
> While Peter was still speaking these words, the Holy Spirit fell upon all those who heard the word. And the circumcised believers who traveled with Peter were amazed that the gift of the Holy Spirit had been poured out upon the Gentiles.
>
> "Can anyone withhold water from these people, who like us have received the Holy Spirit, to be baptized?" (Acts 10:34–35, 44–45, 47; in Thomas A. Wayment, *The New Testament: A Translation for Latter-day Saints*)

It is to me a universal truth that every expansion of our ability to understand that all are alike unto God is a source of both joy and thanksgiving. We love Him even more as the scales fall from our eyes to see in ever-greater clarity that His love is unqualified, that to Him we are all individuals, rather than members of groups or classes of people.

I had thought of myself as a person free of racism because of the wonderful friendships I have enjoyed throughout my life with people of color. But I realized one day, in shame, that an internal dialogue sometimes runs through my mind that sees groups of people, rather than individuals. That day, driving in New York City, I was watching someone saunter across a street ignoring both traffic signals and marked crossings, seeming to enjoy causing traffic to stop for him. And an unvoiced thought ran through my mind, "I wonder if doing this gives *those people* a feeling of power that they lack in other aspects of their lives?" It brought me up short: I would be ashamed to say "those people" out loud, so why would such a thought occur to me? I realized that although I may have acted without racism, my heart and mind had not abandoned prejudices. In that moment, as I prayed for forgiveness, I also prayed that the Lord would help me to overcome all subtle feelings of differences between me and anyone else. The source of those feelings is pride, of course, and a fearful need to feel better than someone else in some way. "There is no fear in love; but perfect love casteth out fear: because fear hath torment. He that feareth is not made perfect in love" (1 John 4:18).

Seeking the gift of charity means letting go of fear *and* of pride. I have found that gratitude can't coexist with fear. So, as I work to be more aware of the incredible array of blessings that a generous Lord has provided me, fear and pride gradually weaken. Like you, I am a work in progress—and that is another source of gratitude for me. I appreciate that a munificent Savior never gives up on me but stands always willing, when sought, to strengthen and comfort, to forgive and forget, to beckon and guide.

There are other opportunities to expand our influence as conduits of Christ's love. I encountered a question posed in a book to which I have often returned: "What is our moral responsibility to other people whom we believe to be wrong, but who desperately need our support and affection?" (Michael Austin, *Re-reading Job: Understanding the Ancient World's Greatest Poem* [2014], 14).

As we seek to follow the example of Jesus Christ, as we pray and work for the gift of charity, how does that influence our associations with others? With those who are our brothers and sisters in an eternal sense, but who may or may not acknowledge Christ as Master and Redeemer? With those who may or may not accept our professions as Christians, or may not welcome any religious or spiritual thought at all?

There have been times in my life when I have felt the sting of rejection simply because of who I am. Sometimes that was because of my being gay, sometimes because of my being a Latter-day Saint. Even though I have had a wonderful life, filled with love and blessings, I also know the feeling of being an outsider, the "other." I know what it means to harbor feelings deep inside that if other people really knew me, they would not choose to be around me. Coping mechanisms that provide protection early in life have to be rooted out later on. I imagine all of us have scars from childhood that need mapping in order to avoid lengthy, unexplained detours in adulthood.

I have learned that even though we may differ in our views of things that are vitally important to us, respect is more easily given after it has been received. I have learned that if I wanted those I loved, friends and associates, to be involved in the things that mattered in my life, I needed to involve myself in theirs. But I couldn't wait for them to act first: I owned that it was my desire to dismantle barriers to understanding and communication, so I needed to reach out again and again, making it as easy as possible for them to reach back.

I have thus come to feel that a constant fixation on earthly fairness for myself is likely the least interesting way to occupy my time (or perhaps it comes a close second to comparing wounds, to see whose trauma has yielded the deepest scars). None of us will emerge from this life unscathed, and our focus is more profitably directed toward Him with Whose stripes we are healed. In the end, the measure of who we have become will be our bettered hearts: how our experiences, our learning from hard knocks and soft embraces, will have caused us to choose over and over again to follow the Giver of the two great commandments of the law.

In Luke we read of "a certain lawyer" who, "willing to justify himself, said unto Jesus, And who is my neighbour?" (Luke 10:25, 29). May I share what is perhaps a modern-day equivalent of Christ's parable of the Good Samaritan? Some time ago, I received an email from a man who had been one of the closest friends to me and to my former partner. In this email, he expressed his bewilderment that I had chosen to be baptized a member of The Church of Jesus Christ of Latter-day Saints. He stated in frank terms his aversion to organized religion, largely because, in his experience, many people of faith seemed hostile to LGBTQ persons.

I wondered how to respond and spent a couple days crafting what I hoped would be a persuasive declaration of my certainty in Christ, my earnest desire to be His disciple, and my hope in continuing revelation, that God will "yet reveal many great and important things"

(Articles of Faith 1:9). His response candidly indicated that my comments had left him unmoved. Despite this lack of understanding and the painful feeling that we had become strangers to one another, over the intervening years, my friend has never stopped reaching out, never flagged in his love, never ceased caring for my welfare and happiness. To paraphrase Jesus's question concluding the parable, "Which now of these, thinkest thou, was neighbour" (Luke 10:36): the one who used careful words to explain his testimony of Christ, or the one who worked tirelessly over a period of years to engage with and care for someone whose motivations he no longer understood?

The experiences of our lives teach us to see the world in a particular way. And yet, in order to truly be of one heart with those around us, to love our neighbors deeply—especially the ones who see and understand the world differently—we have to be willing to think in new ways, to open our minds and our hearts and finally our arms. This is true regardless of any unkindness or contempt they may have shown us.

If our concern is for healing, if our hearts are set on obtaining the gift of charity, then our imperative is for continuous engagement. Only by persistently demonstrating genuine empathy can we rise above a conversation of contention to one centered on sharing where we find meaning in life, our sources of peace and of joy.

What is our moral responsibility to other people whom we believe to be wrong, but who desperately need our support and affection?

In a modern revelation of comfort and promise given to Joseph Smith while a captive in Liberty Jail, the Lord spoke about the exercise of priesthood power. In sharing these words with you, I am changing them slightly to more precisely target our discussion:

No power or influence can or ought to be maintained by virtue of [believing ourselves to be right], only by persuasion, by long-suffering, by gentleness and meekness, and by love unfeigned; By kindness, and pure knowledge, which shall greatly enlarge the soul without hypocrisy, and without guile— Reproving betimes with sharpness, when moved upon by the Holy Ghost; and then showing forth afterwards an increase of love toward him whom thou hast reproved, lest he esteem thee to be his enemy; That he may know that thy faithfulness is stronger than the cords of death. (Doctrine and Covenants 121:41–44)

We need not refrain from stating our case as honestly, as clearly, as thoughtfully, and as respectfully as we can. But might we consider that doing so creates an obligation for us to act with greater love toward those whose beliefs are so different from our own? Can we meet their urgent needs for support and affection without expecting that they will change their views because of our love? Can we hope instead that our hearts and theirs will be changed because we are unwilling to call a brother or sister our enemy or to have them see us in that light?

I believe we must also acknowledge that healing works best in an environment where new wounds are not constantly created, where we have established trust and faithfulness that allow a relationship to thrive even in the face of continued differing views.

What is our moral responsibility to other people whom we believe to be wrong, but who desperately need our support and affection? As President Abraham Lincoln said at the conclusion of his first inaugural address: "We are not enemies, but friends. We must not be enemies. Though passion may have strained, it must not break our

bonds of affection. The mystic chords of memory . . . will yet swell
. . . when again touched, as surely they will be, by the better angels
of our nature" ("First Inaugural Address," Abraham Lincoln Online;
http://www.abrahamlincolnonline.org. Accessed May 23, 2018).

I conclude with a short remembrance. When I was about ten
years old, my family was living in Glenview, Illinois. Our home there
had a two-story living room. The people from whom my parents had
bought the home had left a dieffenbachia plant that was too tall to easily remove. One Sunday afternoon, back in the time when we went to
priesthood meeting and Sunday School in the morning and returned
for sacrament meeting in the evening, my brother Wade decided to
perform a science experiment. Dieffenbachia is also known as "dumb
cane" because the cells of the plant contain raphides, needle-shaped
crystals of calcium oxalate. Wade wanted to see how the plant got its
name. Mom gave him permission to remove one leaf, and Wade carefully biopsied two small sections of the stem. He put one in his mouth
and gave me the other. Wade quickly removed his piece; I gave mine
a good chew. What I didn't realize until afterward is that chewing the
leaf stem causes intense irritation, swelling, and numbing. My tongue
reacted spectacularly, as I recall, making it difficult to swallow and
causing significant pain. An hour or so later, we returned to church. I
was nervous about taking the sacramental bread, fearing that it might
cause me to choke. I chewed it carefully—and it seemed to me that all
the pain and swelling in my mouth went away. The effect of contact
with the raphides is generally of short duration, so some may find my
relief during the sacrament to be merely coincidental. Perhaps so, but
to me, even as a boy, it carried deep and holy meaning.

The gift of charity is enormous in conception, its effect and meaning eternal. And yet, it is also small and intimate and personal, like my experience with dumb cane and the sacrament. The love that we feel from the Savior is all-encompassing, while our sharing of it is often in a measured dose of what an individual needs in the very moment. The greatest expression of Christ's love, His atoning sacrifice, fills the warp and woof of space and time, and yet that sacrifice is also peculiarly, solely for me and for you. Charity requires faith and builds faith. It requires repentance and makes us eager to see that gift also as one of love. Charity grows through revelation and is itself revealed. As we convey our Redeemer's love to others, we are also enveloped in it and grasp how the Father can give all He has to every single son and daughter willing to receive it. Our gratitude for life, and for new life, the perfect isosceles of atonement, resurrection, and exaltation, grows apace with increased knowledge and wisdom: as I better know Father, Son, and Holy Spirit I finally comprehend all Each has given me and the gulf between merit and mercy. As we focus our attention on the two great commandments, the impact and power of our discipleship expand. Through our small daily efforts to attain a new and changed heart, a better heart—one fitted for exaltation—is born.

In all these things we are more than conquerors through him that loved us. For I am persuaded, that neither death, nor life, nor angels, nor principalities, nor powers, nor things present, nor things to come, Nor height, nor depth, nor any other creature, shall be able to separate us from the love of God, which is in Christ Jesus our Lord. (Romans 8:37–39)

Of Him, I am sure.

AFTERWORD

The idea to turn my study of the gift of charity into a book came as a result of invitations to speak at stake and regional devotionals, and especially in my participation with Time Out for Women, which also introduced me to extraordinary presenters and attendees who have enriched my mind and heart. A first step in deciding whether I thought I had anything helpful to offer on the subject was to read what had already been published. The book I most loved in that review, and which I heartily recommend to you, is *A Heart Like His*, by my magnificent friend Virginia Hinckley Pearce.

Laurel Christensen Day was an early champion of this book and read the first manuscript. She provided transformative ideas for improvement and enthusiastic support throughout the whole process. My brothers and sisters-in-law, together with Gerrit and Judy Steenblik and other friends, read the next iteration and gave both encouragement and input, for which I am grateful. Members of the Temple Single Adult Ward were the trial audience for some of the ideas of this book, as well as being exemplars of its principles through their embracing acceptance of all in their circle—including a volunteer class leader.

Much of the final editing of the book took place while I was in London, having the opportunity of a lifetime to work with the sisters and elders of the England London Mission, as a guest of President

David Checketts and Sister Deborah Leishman Checketts. That experience, especially conversation during walks around Hyde Park with Deb and Dave, and the example of each of those missionaries have left their mark on me. My time there was a daily immersion in Christ's pure love.

I am grateful that Deseret Book exists. The team there provides engaging tools for all of us to think more deeply and impetus to learn spiritual truths, as well as creating a platform for an ever-broader range of voices to be heard. This book provided me the opportunity to work again with the incomparable Emily Watts, editor extraordinaire, who generously provided periods and shortened sentences and wielded a scalpel on digressions and overwrought Maxwellisms. Celia Barnes shepherded the book from approval to production with patience and commitment. Sheri Dew, as always, provides insightful questions that drive deeper and better thinking, as well as the gifts of laughter and friendship.

Finally, I want to thank all who took time to write to me, or speak with me, in response to *That We May Be One: A Gay Mormon's Perspective on Faith and Family.* My parents' extraordinary lives have become known to a much wider circle, and I am grateful to all of you for your appreciation of them, as well as for sharing your stories with me. I again express my admiration and love to my family: my brothers, sisters-in-law, my incredible nieces and nephews and their children (and now even the start of a new generation with Ezekiel Thomas Larsen!), and to my Swenson and Christofferson cousins. We stand on the shoulders of giants: the faith, sacrifice, and examples of our parents and grandparents, much like Father Lehi, beckon us to partake of the sweetest fruit, Christ's love.

INDEX

Opportunities, missed, 114–16
Others: poor treatment of, 10–11; respect
for, 14–16; compassion for, 26; caring
for, 37–41; desire to control actions of,
74–75; forgiveness for, 129–30. *See also*
Neighbors; Serving others
Owens, Wayne, 139

Packer, Boyd K., 164
Parable(s): as teaching device, 5; of
Prodigal Son, 5–11, 157–58; of Good
Samaritan, 12–19, 184–85; of Two
Debtors, 48–49, 111; of Ten Virgins,
90–91; of Talents, 91–92; of Sheep and
Goats, 92–93
Parkin, Bonnie D., 114, 134
Passover, 95–98
Paul, 99–100, 124–27, 174
Pearce, Virginia Hinckley, 56–57
Pearson, Carol Lynn, 14–15
Pentecost, 103
Perfection, 137, 175
Perfectionism, 102
Personal revelation, 156–70
Plan of salvation, 145–47, 172
Poor, caring for, 37–41
Power, motivation of, 67–70
Prayer: of Jesus Christ for Nephites, 29–30;
answers to, 55–56; to know if God
knows us, 57–58; of Rabbi Aharon
Davids, 97–98; and repentance, 133
Pride, 63–67, 182–83
Priesthood, celebration of, extended to all
worthy males, 179–81
Priesthood power, exercise of, 185–86
Priests, 13–14
"Private virtuousness," 158
Prodigal Son, parable of, 5–11, 157–58
Progress, spiritual, 116
Punishment, 89
Purposes, as absorbed into actions, 63–64

Questions, 143–45

Racism, 182
Refugees, 42, 80–82
Rejection, 183
Renlund, Dale G., 76, 137–38
Repentance, 33–34, 49, 132–34
Reservoirs, spiritual, 148–49
Respect for others, 14–16
Resurrection, 52–53
Retirement, 169–70
Revelation, personal, 156–70
Revenge, 89
Rich young ruler, 165–66
Righteous Father of Two Sons, allegory
of, 33
Righteousness, 61–62, 66. *See also*
Motive(s)
Rivlin, Reuven, 96–97
Romney, Marion G., 37–38
Russell, Bertrand, 125

Sacrament, 53, 187–88
Saint-Exupéry, Antoine de, 141–43
Sales, 171–72
Salt Lake City Inner City Mission, 152–53
Salt Lake Temple, dedication prayer for,
35–36
Salvation, through Jesus Christ, 16–17,
32–33, 50–51. *See also* Plan of salvation
Samaritan woman at Jacob's Well, 26–27,
174–75
Scott, Richard G., 161–62
Scriptures, and coming unto Christ, 3–5
Second World War, 80–82, 89–90, 95–98,
141–42, 158
Self-disappointment, 136–37
Serving others: and parable of Good
Samaritan, 12–16; influence through,
37–44, 150–51; and Last Supper,
69–70; serving Lord through, 93; and